Letters from Bohemia

Books by Ben Hecht

LETTERS FROM BOHEMIA

GAILY, GAILY

THE SENSUALISTS

PERFIDY

A TREASURY OF BEN HECHT

CHARLIE

CHILD OF THE CENTURY

A GUIDE FOR THE BEDEVILLED

A BOOK OF MIRACLES

ACTORS BLOOD

CHAMPION FROM FAR AWAY

A JEW IN LOVE

1001 AFTERNOONS IN NEW YORK

BROKEN NECKS

COUNT BRUGA

I HATE ACTORS

THE KINGDOM OF EVIL

HUMPTY DUMPTY

1001 AFTERNOONS IN CHICAGO

FANTAZIUS MALLARE

GARGOYLES

ERIK DORN

Letters from Bohemia

by BEN HECHT

*   *
*

1964
DOUBLEDAY & COMPANY, INC.
GARDEN CITY, NEW YORK

Grateful acknowledgment is made for permission to use material by the following persons:

Anderson, Sherwood — reprinted by permission of Mrs. Sherwood Anderson.

Antheil, George — reprinted by permission of Mrs. George Antheil.

Fowler, Gene — reprinted by permission of Mrs. Gene Fowler.

Grosz, George — reprinted by permission of Peter M. Grosz, Co-executor of the Estate of George and Eva Grosz.

MacArthur, Charles — reprinted by permission of Mrs. Charles MacArthur.

Mencken, Henry Louis — reprinted by permission of Mercantile-Sale Deposit and Trust Company, Trustee of the Estate of Henry Louis Mencken.

Library of Congress Catalog Card Number 64–16207
Printed in the United States of America
First Edition

CONTENTS

1. About Fowler   11

2. About Mencken   67

3. About Sherwood Anderson   85

4. About Bodenheim   105

5. About Grosz   133

6. About Antheil   155

7. About MacArthur   183

Letters from Bohemia

BULLETIN FROM THE COAST
OF BOHEMIA

The writers of the letters in this book had one thing in common — they were artists. Varying degrees of fame rewarded their efforts but they were as identical as spring lambs in the pastures of art.

I pause to nod apology to their gravestones, for my old friends when alive would have snorted at the word "artists." They might even have resented "spring lambs." Indeed, Fowler changed the title of his last autobiographical book, *Skyline*. He had dubbed it first, *The Odyssey of a Spring Lamb*.

My friends were touchy fellows. They worked like cart horses to become artists but insisted on being regarded as solid citizens. Artists are often like that; in fact, I have known no other. However violent their protests against society, they are always eager to shine as well-mannered, pleasingly clothed members of the community. Nonconformity is as embarrassing to the "true artist" (meaning one of genuine talent and lush productivity) as nudity. His mind may be fearless of attracting attention, but his person shies from it as from a head cold.

My seven correspondents were all wild men in print, in music or on canvas. But you couldn't have bribed one of them to indulge publicly in an unconventional antic, when sober. They preened themselves on being men who enjoyed playing cards, drinking schnapps, mooning around with girls, driving automobiles, living in good houses with their families, and voting for public officials.

This is not an entirely authentic picture of them. Anderson, Grosz, Bodenheim, and Mencken could no more drive a car than swim the Hellespont. None of them, except Mac-Arthur, knew the ins and outs of any card game; and Mac-Arthur was a Simple Simon at a card table. He played with ferocity, always lost, and the cards kept falling out of his large fingers as if he were practicing juggling.

Fowler, who knew scores of noted gamblers, never, to my knowledge, placed a bet on anything. I saw him in many sporting activities, including whale hunts off the coasts of Fire Island and Santa Monica; including, also, a fracas in a Los Angeles hotel dining room. There, with the aid of Roland Brown, he scattered the back field of the visiting Notre Dame football team. Some insults had been passed by the hefty collegians over Gene's ordering of a fourth pot of tea, a sobriety gesture in honor of his wife Agnes, who was at his side.

Swing his fists, race a car, harpoon leviathans, but I have no memory of Fowler with a pair of dice or a deck of cards in his hand.

As for voting, it is my impression that the only one of my correspondents who ever cast a ballot was MacArthur. At least, he once tried to argue me into voting for General Eisenhower, and I deduce he may have done so himself.

The liquoring part of the picture is more authentic. They were all industrious drinkers, except Anderson who was a wine sipper. A lone glass of booze would set him to singing barn dance ditties and sliding out of his seat.

Poet Bodenheim was the star drinker of the lot. Picked up unconscious from a Bleecker Street gutter and carted off to the alcoholic ward of Bellevue Hospital, he murmured as he came out of his two-day coma, "I must have had a drop too much." Until the age of sixty, when he had his head blown off by a demented sailor, our poet's words were always undaunted.

Bogie (his Chicago nickname) looked down on Mac-

Arthur and Fowler as drinkers, despite their well-earned reputations.

"It is child's play to become intoxicated," said the poet, "if your pockets are always bulging with greenbacks, as are Mr. MacArthur's and Mr. Fowler's. I would like to see how far they would get if they had to steal their alcoholic beverages as I have more often than not been forced to do. Mr. Mencken, who is constantly informing his readers of his libations, is a total fraud. He drinks beer, a habit no more bacchanalian than taking enemas."

About the conventionality of my friends as husbands and lovers, I invoke the Fifth Amendment.

Socially, my correspondents were all Emily Post "alumni." They said "yes, sir" and "no, sir" to strangers, removed their hats in elevators, haunted barbershops, kept their teeth in good repair, and allowed lady friends to precede them through doorways. Except Anderson. Swatty (his Chicago nickname) insisted he had more important things on his mind than such niceties as "who goes first."

To make up for this small unconventionality, Sherwood always bowed slightly when being introduced to a girl, and dressed up in dark cheviot suits like a European financier.

There were several reasons for my friends' finickiness about being hailed as "artists," modesty being the least of them. The word "artists" offered a picture of fellows with odd haircuts who were partial to floors rather than chairs as sitting places. Such characters, abounding in the larger cities, relished being thought "different." They proclaimed themselves by beards, sandals, sheepskin jackets, and unemployment as being Bohemians or free souls. If they continued after adolescence to favor tight pants and hobo romances, and refused snobbishly to write, paint, or compose anything salable, they acquired the title, artist. They found a peculiar status in looking down on success as bourgeoise and belittling.

There was another picture suggested by the word "artist"

that was equally disturbing. In addition to being impoverished zanies who were often found frozen to death in their garrets, "artists" were also people who were enormously overpaid for playing the fiddle, piano, or cornet, for making faces in front of movie cameras, for cracking jokes on coast-to-coast programs, and so forth. The public is given to such paradoxes, and remains, somehow, unconfused by them.

My correspondents never got a toe into this category. Even Anderson, who became internationally famous, remained wary of picking up a dinner tab. They were all, except Bodenheim, well off, which meant that they managed to die without being evicted from their homes or going to jail for debt. Fowler used to call himself "the giled pauper." Mencken said, "If I stopped working for a month, I would land in Skid Row." MacArthur, two of whose brothers were millionaires, took several fliers in the Stock Market and ended up working a double shift in the Hollywood salt mines.

I remember numerous incidents and conversations having to do with their aversion to the identity of "artist." My friends, tireless producers of art in words, music, and paint, never discussed their own work. They snorted considerably at other men's art efforts. But of their own dreams and products — nothing.

Except Anderson. If a girl was with us, I was sure to hear Swatty open up as a searcher for deep truths. You could tell how smitten he was with a girl by how ardently he started praising himself. He called it "self-revelation."

Bodenheim, when in his cups, contented himself with announcing, "poetry is the impish attempt to paint the color of the wind."

Bodenheim, sunk to the bottom of Greenwich Village, once sneered at a policeman who was dragging him off to the station house, "Your ignorance is a blustering uniform. I am not a drunken artist, but an intoxicated Communist, a Red wino. Put that in your pipe and smoke it."

George Grosz, the wildest Aryan painting talent to escape Hitler's Germany, used to try to sound like an ambassador, even when talking to his intimates, "The City of St. Louis is, if I may say so, not an ideal metropolis. In fact, one might say, it is not quite habitable. Forgive me for sounding maybe too critical but I am speaking only as an outsider; a man, shall we say, from the fifteenth century, anno Domini."

When Anderson worked in Chicago as an "idea man" for the advertising firm of Taylor-Critchfield and Company, and was having his *Winesberg, Ohio* short stories rejected by New York magazine editors as if they were subpoenas he was trying to serve on them, our great iconoclast would leave a party if anybody showed up minus a tie, or wearing sandals without socks. He did not care to be caught among "those goddamn artists out of the Funny Papers."

Antheil, whose *Ballet Mécanique* called for an orchestra including two high-powered airplane propellers, six mechanical player pianos, twelve electric door bells in working order, ten massive drums, and four large tin washtubs to be beaten with croquet mallets, Georgie would wince at the sight of a musician with long hair; and have nothing to do with a girl who wasn't a good cook.

During the New York performance of *Ballet Mécanique* in Carnegie Hall, music critic De Vries affixed a white handkerchief to the tip of his walking stick and waved it frantically from his mezzanine box. After the concert was over, Antheil who had conducted it said indignantly, "I saw Mr. De Vries waving his handkerchief in surrender. I thought it was a very unconventional thing for a critic to do."

While casting a movie, MacArthur received the photograph of a ballerina as an applicant for the starring role. The dancer was nude. Her large rear was turned to the camera and her face beamed over her shoulder. Under her name was the printed information, "Czechoslovakia's Greatest Artist."

"That word covers too much territory," said MacArthur.

Antheil shook his head at the photograph. "That's a confusing word," he said. "Ezra Pound wrote a book about me in which he called me a great artist, and almost everybody I knew started trying to borrow money from me."

Grosz once said, his sharp features aglow with slivovitz, "At a very early age I began to suspect I was, what you might call, an artist, due to the fact the young ladies I knew preferred to go out with other fellows."

"That is because women know instinctively that artists are not looking for happiness," said Titus Tautz, co-chairman of the Dadaists in Germany, where this conversation took place.

"Do you, my dear friend," Grosz asked, "happen to know what the artist is looking for?"

"Not remotely," said the gifted Tautz.

"Very good, I agree," said Grosz, "and the important thing is he must never find it. He will become, then, only a successful man."

Mencken said, after a fourth bottle of home-brewed beer (it was Prohibition time), "I don't know what an artist is, but I know damn well what he isn't — a bore."

Said Fowler, "I guess I'll never be considered an artist due to having reached the ripe age of sixty without hating anyone or anything — in print.

         ✦   ✦   ✦

But I'll let the word "artist" stand as their true name. Being six feet underground, all of them, my correspondents are incapable of rebuttal. *There's* a thing that keeps surprising you about stormy old friends after they die — their silence. For a while an echo stays in your ear. You hear a laugh, a knowing phrase or two, a certain quality of enunciation. Then, nothing. Another death takes place — voices.

This is the technique of mortality — everything must vanish to make way for new things. The theory is that the dead souls float off into some roomier heaven. I have not given much thought to this matter. It is difficult enough identifying the straggling realities of life, without trying to give shape and meaning to death. I concluded, when young, that my opinions of the hereafter were of no consequence, would have no influence on it, and were unnecessary to my well-being as an earthling. I remained, however, interested. My correspondents (except Mencken) were full of some sort of conviction of life after death. Nearly all of them, particularly Fowler, promised to get in touch with me if I was still around after their obsequies.

Not Mencken. Sitting in a saloon one evening, Mencken said, "The biggest hoax perpetrated by the human mind is its 'life after death' valentine."

I asked him if he was sure. He said he was.

But the others — not a table rap from one of them, not a ghostly cackle in the night; nothing.

"One of the reasons I've joined the Catholic Church," Fowler informed me one evening in Hollywood, "is that I feel convinced that if anybody carries a reporter's press-card in the Great Beyond, he's likely to be a Catholic. My intentions, once I pass the Pearly Gates, are to present my Papal credentials, interview the proper Personages or Forces, and get the story back to our blindfolded planet. You know, I've always been a good reporter."

He was — the best newspaperman ever to caper through our old profession.

"You may expect a full report from me," Fowler said, "the first tidings from the valley of the shadow of death. I always got a story back."

As far as I know, Fowler muffed this one. I've heard not a peep out of him. Or out of MacArthur, another agile newsman once.

"Keep your ears open," MacArthur instructed me on one of his last days, "I may have some surprising things to tell you."

When I was writing a book about MacArthur (*Charlie*) I lay awake nights certain that my old collaborator would pop into the room with some tidy criticism. On several occasions, I fancied I saw him. He appeared for a few moments and stuck his head out of the opened window and looked at the Hudson River as he used to do when we were writing plays or movies together, and had hit a snag.

But I knew it was no visitor from the other side. He was a ghost out of my own head, which has become as full of them as a Halloween party.

One wintry afternoon in my house, Bodenheim, almost at the end of his rope, said,

"I believe there is a God. And I believe that He is somewhat interested in improving His inventions after they have died and returned to His workshop. Yes, I believe in future improvements, especially for poets — who have found life exquisitely deficient."

No voices have sounded. My dead friends have stayed uncharacteristically silent. Only their books, music, and paintings speak for them. And here, in the following pages, are some letters they wrote to me before they vanished.

As a preface to each small or large batch of letters I shall relate some anecdotes of their writers. There will be no research in these tales but an exercise only in memory. Conversations, incidents — if they seem peculiar, you should remember that peculiarity is the mark of the artist, however trim and polite he may seem. As Sherwood used to say, the artist is someone who answers back. He didn't mean that he was full of protest against what went on in the world, but full of performance.

A few years before his death, Mencken asked me if I cared to write some two or three thousand words about him. He was making a similar request of twenty other writers with whom he had been friendly. The articles, he explained, would be published in a book after his demise. Such a book, he felt, would be an ideal biography of him.

I sent Mencken my piece about him. Some months later he wrote me, "Of the eighteen articles I have received from my friends, only yours and two others were about me. The other fifteen were about the doings and unrest of their authors, and had practically nothing to do with me. It is, as I have long suspected, very difficult for a writer to write about anybody but himself. I have abandoned my plan for any posthumous pen-portrait."

Mencken was right. It isn't easy to remember others more vividly than oneself. But I shall try to write less of myself than of my seven dead friends who, in a fashion, molded much of my life — Gene Fowler, Sherwood Anderson, H. L. Mencken, Maxwell Bodenheim, George Grosz, George Antheil, and Charles MacArthur.

At least, their letters will contribute firmly to their portraits.

About Fowler

TALE OF THE FALSE CORPSE

"He says it's Charles MacArthur of the *Examiner*," said Jimmy Coogan, head copy boy on the Chicago *Daily News*, "and he says it's imperative that he talk to you at once."

"The police," said MacArthur over the phone, "are holding a rather interesting fellow captive in the East Harrison Street bull pen. His name is Gene Fowler, which seems to be an alias."

It was. As a child Fowler had soothed his grandmother's feelings by substituting her name for his runaway daddy's name of Devlin.

MacArthur continued, "He's a journalist making his way from Denver to New York in peculiar fashion—chaperoning a corpse. Under the law the undertaker has to provide a live attendant for every traveling cadaver. The charge on the police blotter against alias Gene Fowler is treason."

"The police can't arrest anybody for treason," I said, "the federal government has to do that."

"Very good, Brainy Bowers," said MacArthur, "but I just had a chat with Captain Strassneider. He says it's treason. I'm opposed to a fellow newspaperman falling before a firing squad."

I agreed to try to help stay the execution of the Denver émigré, Gene Fowler.

It was a summer afternoon in 1917. I remember Charlie's face, young as my own. On the way to Harrison Street, I learned that our Western colleague had been touring for some time with his casket. It contained the mortal remains of a female, my memory wavers between a Whistler's Mother or a Magdalene. But whatever was in the box, escort

Fowler had changed its identity to that of a heroic French colonel who had been wounded recently on the Marne and come to Colorado to die. There must have been some reason for the French hero's migration, but it is out of reach.

Wrapping the hero's coffin in the French tricolor, Fowler had zigzagged from Denver to New Orleans, to Chicago; eager to behold the arcs of his native land for the first time, with a distracted undertaker footing the bill.

Fowler had also made stop-overs in smaller cities, after telegraphing their mayors of the great French hero who was coming their way.

Voilà — bands had played at Midwestern depots, orations had been delivered over the flag-draped box. Fowler had been wined and dined and coaxed into offering a word picture of how and where the dead hero had given up the ghost in the first great war against militarism.

"I'll tell you just what this Fowler sonofabitch did," said Captain Strassneider in his East Harrison Street office. "He checked his phony corpse at the La Salle Street Station, after convincing the baggage master the coffin was full of rare books the City of Denver was sending as a gift to the New York Public Library. Then this Fowler sashayed around the Loop for several hours, and finally came to the Morrison Hotel. He was standing at the desk registering his alias, Gene Fowler, when he suddenly stops and lets out a yell that paralyzed the lobby.

"You know that fifteen-foot American flag made out of red, white, and blue electric lights that's at the rear of the lobby?" Captain Strassneider asked.

"A beautiful display of Americanism," said MacArthur.

"Well, this traitor, Fowler, lets out an unheard of stream of profanity when he sees it," said Captain Strassneider. "We got a score of witnesses. He knocks over two bell boys and the house dick who try to restrain him. He rushes at that American flag. He picks up the large gold fish bowls that stand at each end of the flag. And he throws the gold fish bowls at the flag, breaking half its electric lights. Then he tries to kick out the remaining electric lights of the flag before he is overpowered.

"And," said the captain, "if that ain't treason, I'd like to know what is!"

Our next stop was the East Harrison Street bull pen. There, standing gracefully amid a crush of white and colored thugs, pimps, whores, drunks, and hop heads was our Denver colleague. A tall young man, a few years older than us; large hands hanging beside long legs; a sort of good-looking hatchet face featuring a pair of merry eyes (gray). But his outstanding quality was his voice. It said, "hello" like a man trying out the echoes in a cave. It rose from lower "g" to middle "c" and descended back to "g," giving the effect of two men speaking; two polite and gallant men who were mocking each other.

I had known voices of this sort, but never as full blown and distinctive. Their purr of deference belonged usually to men who were quick to swing their fists.

In those days I had a theory that I could tell in an hour what a man would be forever. The theory failed me frequently, but not with Fowler. What I thought on first espying him, I still thought when I helped carry his oaken coffin some forty years later to its Los Angeles grave. A man of genius, wit, and high-toned attitudes was loose in the world.

I have lost the details of how we pried Fowler out of police clutches. I imagine we found a couple of free phones and did a lot of telephoning. Despite our youth and poverty, we could speak with the voices of Mr. Hearst's *Examiner* and Mr. Victor Lawson's *Daily News*, voices that could coax or blackmail good deeds out of most of the whiskey-nosed dignitaries of the City Hall and County Building.

But I remember Fowler, the day after his release, in Lincoln Park. The three of us sat on a bench and watched some five hundred Indians shooting bows and arrows and leaping around in war bonnets. They were part of the Dearborn Centennial Celebration; re-enacting, to the delight of thousands of Chicagoans, the massacre of Fort Dearborn's men, women, and children a century ago.

"It's a stirring sight," said Fowler in his slide-trombone voice. "Too bad it's all in fun."

He held a flask to his lips until it was empty.

"Yes, sir," he continued moodily, "my recent experiences with my traveling companion — that would-be French hero — have left me with some doubts about the White Man. Judging from the orations I heard, patriotism seems to fill his head with sewer gas. You gentlemen have been kind enough not to inquire why I sought to destroy our National Emblem in the hotel lobby. I'll tell you — because it was made out of electric lights. A false display, sirs, like the Golden Calf set up by the confused Hebrews in their trek to the Promised Land. I feel it would be better to return our country to these handsome savages from whom we stole it, than to become an American serving under an Electric Light. I hope I make myself clear."

"Yes," said MacArthur, opening a fresh bottle, "advertisement conquers all in our land, including the Stars and Stripes."

TALE OF THE SUICIDE STROLL

In New York City some years later, Fowler and I put MacArthur to bed in the Algonquin Hotel. Our Charles had run into some new troubles in his Homeric campaign to divorce his first wife, Carol Frink, to be able, thus, to marry the young actress, Helen Hayes, who filled his heart and his dreams. And who was to remain enthroned therein for some thirty years of subsequent marriage. But this fine future was hidden from our friend as we removed his shoes for a night's rest.

In the sitting room of our suite, Fowler opened a bottle, filled a tumbler with whiskey, and spoke as he paced his swallows.

"I am a happily married man," he said, "and a grateful one. Agnes [his wife] is unique among women. She has not only put up with me and presented me with three offspring, but admired me during the rain of shrapnel in which we have been living since our honeymoon.

"Our pal Snooker" — this was Fowler's invented name for MacArthur — "made the mistake of marrying the first woman he loved. Miss Frink, her name is, is it not?"

I nodded.

"It is a disastrous thing to do," said Fowler, "rush to the altar with the first wench who clouds your reason. I, fortunately, did not. As a result I am a happy husband without a police record. And I have a lifetime loving mate at my side, instead of a short-run Venus with an expensive lawyer blighting my day, as has befallen Snooker.

"But I do not owe my good fortune to any intelligence of my own," continued Fowler. "When I remember my first male yearning for disaster, I am ready to forgive any man his sins, providing they are based on his stupidity."

The Fowler cadences went on but I'll tell them rather than quote them. For much liquor was consumed that night and I emerged from it with a haze of facts more than a bundle of words. In the next thirty years, Fowler's story that night remained a constant part of my knowledge of him. I asked him often if he ever intended to write the story in a book. He would shake his head and say he had forgotten it too much to try to get any literary mileage out of it.

One summer, however, he came to live in my house in Nyack while Rose and I were away in Hollywood. With only our garden and our French poodle, Gogol, for company,

Gene wrote the story he had told me in the Algonquin suite where Snooker tossed in pain. He permutated and transposed the tale, considerably; hid it in another civilization and darkened the skin of its characters. But it was the same story, nevertheless. It was called *Illusion in Java*. I still think it one of the most sensitive novels in the world's literature of man and woman love.

The story Gene told in the hotel happened in his Denver youth. After a sort of Robinson Crusoe childhood that had included running errands for the town's bawdy house madams, our hero had shot up into a tall, gangly moneyless reporter, given to spending his nights as if he were a one-man revival of the Old West. And during this time of liquoring, fist fighting (once with his townsman, Jack Dempsey), and news gathering, young Fowler met a girl. Or rather, a representative of the opposite sex came rolling into his heart like an avalanche.

I have some theories about love that concern me as well as Fowler. I won't expand on them, for who, in this era of literature about females whose legs fly open like trick compasses, cares to hear of love with its clothes on; of love as sexless as levitation or some other great feat of magic.

Love that does not send the male hand ferreting under a dress, that turns him into a castrate such as the angels in heaven are said to be; that transplants the male heart into the prettier bosom of a female, and leaves him gored like a picador's horse — my theory about this love is that it is, (partly) the giddy, impractical desire of a man to become both man and woman; not exactly a hermaphrodite but a creature finer and more complex than the rutting male. He lives not in himself, but in the woman he loves. Her smiles, tears, whispers, sighs, wishes, are, mysteriously, his own. If she looks unhappy he is likely to die. If she laughs, he leaps into heaven. He has, actually, no existence of his own. His beloved is his reality.

I said, "partly." This abstracted gelding can write poetry,

make plans like a Crusader after Saladin, and continue his routines among common folk; not too well, but sufficient to remain employed.

Young Fowler's love for his Denver Juliet was of this kind. Except that it lacked the crudeness of Shakespeare who, possibly to please his vulgar audiences, bedded his lyric Romeo with his heroine. A man in love like Romeo can no more join his beloved between the sheets than push his dear mother off a roof; at least, not for some time.

She was young, radiant, and lived in a glittering house behind an ornamental iron fence. Her Capulet parents were among the wealthiest in the City, and the leaders of its Society. They owned horses and automobiles. Butlers, gardeners, cooks and frilly capped maids abounded in their domain. And there was a rival suitor, a young man of great social distinction whose parents owned a chain of silver mines in Colorado. They may have been copper ones. My reporter's mind is hazed over, as I said, concerning the exact details of the story Fowler told in that booze-flowing night in our hotel suite.

But I remember this — young Fowler loved with no more chance of winning the girl than of getting elected President of the United States. Her parents shooed him from their premises, and set up road blocks for their infatuated daughter. Yes, indeed, the girl was as swooning for Fowler as he was for her. She met him in clandestine trysts, wept in his arms, cried out her eternal love — and returned, pale and wobbling, to the glittering house behind the ornamental iron fence.

At the height of this monsoon courtship, Fowler received a summons from his beloved's father to the hitherto forbidden Capulet home. Shaved, his best pants pressed, his hair reeking of bay rum, young Fowler entered an extensive drawing room. Its splendors numbed him.

"Sit down, Gene," said the room's other occupant, father of his beloved. "What will you have to drink, sir?"

"I have given up liquor," young Fowler answered, a statement I have remembered because of its novelty. For Gene assured me that it was true. He had not once sullied his passion for his Juliet by dousing it with a drop of booze.

Whereupon, the father spoke to the liquorless Fowler in such a fashion as sank a spear into his heart and slew all its dreams. His lovely daughter, he said, had been born in a world of riches, reared in it; danced and reveled sweetly in it; been covered all her life with silks, laces, gems, and furs; been attended all her life by doting servitors. She had never so much as boiled an egg or dusted a mantelpiece. She was, in short, a Princess, trained only to enjoy luxuries, idleness, and glamorous social diversions.

And what, asked this father, would happen to such a young woman if she were replanted in a shabby house in which she had to cook, scrub floors, wash dishes and clothes, wear cotton dresses, and never come near a grand piano on which to play Bach and Mozart. All this would befall the wife of a newspaperman earning thirty dollars a week, and with not a nickel in the bank or a stock or bond to his name.

Such a girl as his daughter would be totally destroyed. Her bloom would vanish. She would sit among her pots and pans like someone in exile. And so forth . . .

It is a speech out of many an old drama, usually greeted with snorts or hisses by democratic audiences. But it was Fowler who heard it. If there was one basic thing about young or old Fowler, it was his horror of bringing hurt to anyone. He would rather have lost an arm than bring pain to a fellow human. Of course, he hurt quite a few humans, more of one sex than another; and kept both his arms. But his remorse for any such misdeed nigh eviscerated him. Until he joined the Catholics, in his fifties, the only penance he knew was to drown his sins in liquor.

"What does your daughter think of this foul future into which I seem to be luring her?" young Fowler asked.

He was told that his beloved had agreed to take a six-month cruise around the world. On her return she would be allowed to decide whether she wished to marry one of her own kind (the silver-mine aristocrat) or a newspaper Ned in a world of unwashed dishes.

"I think," said Fowler, "she has already decided."

"I'll be fair," said the father, "she's upstairs at the moment sobbing her heart out, for you, sir. You can wreck my plans for her, and still destroy her — if you so choose."

Young Fowler rose, bowed and walked, shakenly, out of the drawing room of splendor, and out of his beloved's life. Neither MacArthur nor I would have favored this plot turn. But neither of us was Fowler. Though we seemed alike in numerous ways, we lacked the Healer's soul that was Fowler's; the fear of hurting others by our desires. Or, maybe, the lack was in Fowler. He was a mite too much devoid of ego.

But not of emotion. The young Fowler who walked through the ornamental iron gates and left behind his princess, had only one thought in his head — suicide. But how does a proud young man kill himself, without seeming like a horse's ass to his city desk, and his fellow newspapermen, his coterie of bartenders, prize fighters, old prospector coots, and other such critical confreres?

An answer came to young Fowler. He would put his life down as a chip and gamble for it. In my memory, the scene moves to a tall hotel. It is a windy night. Young Fowler sits in one of the rooms on the tenth floor. A last liquor bottle has been emptied. He is ready for the gamble.

Up he stands, without sway in him. Fowler was never of those who sway in their cups. Liquor seemed only to effect his imagination. It filled him with curious ambitions and sent him off on peculiar projects.

This night in the tall hotel, Fowler walks to the window, opens it, and steps out on the two-foot ledge that circles the hotel, as an ornamental token. He steps out on the ledge, and starts his gambler's pilgrimage. The rules of the game are as follows — he will walk around the entire goddamn hotel on the two-foot ledge ten stories above the street. If God, the howling wind, and the liquor in his blood so will it, he will fall from the ledge into the far-below street. And there will be an end to his pain of lost love. But he will walk as carefully as he can, like a man honorably intent on returning to the opened window of his hotel room.

Thus young Fowler walked. I recall little of his description of his suicide stroll, but having known him well I can see him. A bitterness in his eyes and, nevertheless, a grin on his young face. I can imagine the befuddled exultation in his soul. It was always in him when he went adventuring.

"I made the grand tour on the ledge," said Fowler, "and returned to my quarters without knowing quite if I had won or lost."

The story has a happy ending. I remember many of its words.

"A few months later," said Fowler, "I met a wonderful girl with a sweet face and a great deal of spirit. I married her, good Agnes. A lady who would not wither but bloom at my side, who would smile at poverty, and love my lumbering, incompetent ways. The love pain for the lost Juliet? I'll tell you about it. A few years later I received a letter from my first Denver love with a request in it. Would I meet her in the lobby of the Biltmore Hotel in Los Angeles? She had a matter of great importance to communicate.

"I met her. She was married to the aristocratic mine owner but was intent now on divorcing him. She would be free in a few months. And was I still interested in her.

"I listened to every word and all I could hear was a strange female talking preposterously. I recalled my walk around the ledge, but decided not to tell her about it. I felt I couldn't explain the incident. So help me God, I couldn't have explained it either to her, or to myself. All

I could think of as I looked on the somewhat fragile young matron was, thank God for Agnes."

MacArthur woke around noon, and demanded food. His face was grim with decision. He announced he was going to try to borrow enough money to travel to Chicago and bribe his clinging Carol to divorce him. Should bribery fail, he would turn into a new Bluebeard and terrorize her into submission.

"I'm going to marry Helen," said MacArthur, "if I have to wade to her side, knee deep in blood."

Hearing Charlie's laments, I thought that Fowler's gamble on the hotel ledge had been a wiser way of dealing with a first love than taking it to the altar. But when I read *Illusion in Java*, I wondered if wisdom had any place in such a dilemma.

Although my friend Fowler was a happy man in many ways and full of much content and devotion, I wondered if he had ever gotten off that ledge around the hotel. Or if all of him had crawled back into the window of his hotel room on that windy night.

THE PINWHEEL OF NEW YORK

Fowler wrote a number of books about his doings in New York. They are books full of gusto and anecdote, with never a lie in them, except of omission.

The omission was chiefly Fowler. Modesty tripped up his pen. He could write exuberantly of his friends, and fill his pages with bird calls concerning their wild hearts and exotic antics. But of himself, hardly a hint. He was unable even to do the Hemingway trick of turning himself into a third person hero of a novel.

And who shall say it is wrong for a writer to practice

modesty in print? And even tolerance? That was another Fowler addiction as a writer. He could write no ill word of anyone. In life he could roar with rage, wreck buildings, break jaws and noses. But in print—an amiable man beamed on all he saw; a happy wit piped all hands to a gay party.

As a result Fowler left behind a bouncy record of scores of characters, and little of himself. I have reread Gene's books since he died, and I felt remiss. It seemed to me I had never praised Gene enough for his volumes.

They will come into style some day when the public becomes fed up with the sickly probings of our modern literateurs; with the cultish swagger of Hemingway, the murky broodings of Faulkner, the beanbag games of Salinger. Fed up, also, with the itemizing of the defeats of life and pulling a long face as a mark of higher endeavor.

The day will come when a decadence-bored public will gratefully embrace Fowler's healthy and ribald reports of his time. And Fowler will then take his rightful place in the ranks of Steinbeck, O'Hara, Lardner, and Twain.

I do not expect to undo Fowler's modesty in the few pages of his life in New York I have to offer. I can put down no more than a few hints of my adventurous and magnetic friend. Even so, he may visit me as he once promised, not with revelations but with chidings.

The principal note about Fowler was his popularity. Not a celebrity's popularity. But the grin and hello of people who knew him. And what a Noah's Ark of them there were. Spending an evening in town with Fowler was like chumming it with some Pied Piper (no jape intended.)

People popped out of pool halls, saloons, hotel doors; darted across streets and came hallooing out of gyms, taxi cabs, theatre lobbies—all to hail "their boy, Gene." Moochers, winos, out-of-work newspapermen, bartenders, actors knew him well, and he knew them. And emptied his thin wallet into their hands, year on year.

It's a dubious thing to say of a friend, but there was a saintliness to Fowler. His sophisticated friends insisted it was all a pose. I thought so myself, at times. What logical reason was there for a busy, hard-up writer to dole out so much time, money, and deep concern to a pack of useless people? But it was no pose. It's no pose when you see a man shell out fifty dollars to a washed-up prize fighter, and then go humble himself borrowing half of it back from some solvent acquaintance, so that Agnes and his brood might buy food over the weekend.

Once in a hotel room, Fowler visited his friend Larney Lichtenstein, the prize fighters' manager. Larney was a short, chubby gentleman in a comedian's overcoat of red, green, and black checkered material.

"You're looking a little peaked," said Larney to Gene.

"He's in a little financial trouble," I explained. Gene frowned at me but not so Larney. Manager Larney pulled a roll of bills out of his pocket, and started riffling them as if they were a pack of cards.

"Say when," Larney said.

Fowler's popularity was not only among the washouts of the town. He knew every judge, lawyer, and police official of note; knew all the fight champions, their managers and sweethearts; knew the stars of the theatre, its producers, press agents and backers; knew a slue of cafe owners, renowned gangsters and bootleggers; famous surgeons, scientists, Wall Street financiers. And they knew him, with a special camaraderie, an eagerness for his presence: Tex Rickard, the Marx Brothers, Jack Dempsey, David Belasco, Arthur Hopkins, Tommy Hitchcock, Herbert Swope, Jack Curley, Owney Madden, Al Smith, Arch Selwyn, Jack Barrymore, Judge Landis, Red Skelton, Mayor Walker, Billy Rose, Wilson Mizner, Queen Marie of Roumania, Jimmy Durante, Flo Ziegfeld, W. R. Hearst, Babe Ruth, Attorney Leibowitz, Dewey, O'Dwyer, Wild Bill Donovan, Teddy Roosevelt — there's no end to the listing.

What was the Fowler attraction? Wit and laughter always on tap, but more, a sense of excitement that emanated from him.

There was only one social set in which Fowler had no existence, the set of literary folk. I think MacArthur and I were the only two writers he knew for many years.

He refused to come lunch at the Round Table in the Algonquin Hotel where Alexander Woollcott, Heywood Broun, Robert Benchley, George S. Kaufman, Marc Connelly, and other men of letters gathered daily to discuss poker losses and new illnesses.

Fowler paled at the prospect of sitting among such fancy folk as if he were some Ragged Dick bid to a minuet. Pressed to explain his reluctance, he said, "They are critics, each and every one of them. I always get the heaves in the presence of critics, especially Eastern ones."

What he didn't say was that he had an aversion for the punster wit and coy bon mots of most of the Round Table coterie. Also, he was not deft at exchanging verbal insults, a vital part of the Table's conversaziones. His face and fists were likely to tighten at any slur, however artfully phrased.

Hoping one year to blast his way into solvency, Fowler decided to take on the side line of prize fight manager. Tex Rickard promised him his Madison Square Garden for any heavyweight contender he might produce.

A month later Fowler had imported a powerful slugger from South Africa, Johnny Squires. Gene put him up in a hotel room and began filling the town's sports pages with startling tales of his protégé.

Fighter Squires had refused to get into condition due to the absence of his trainer who was signaling morosely from South Africa.

"He's my other self," said the pugilist, "I'm nothin' without him to guide me."

Fowler, at dizzying expense, brought his fighter's alter ego to New York. He was a little man full of complaints. Lying down in the fighter's bed, he explained to Fowler that he was suffering from an ulcer, and was also a victim of insomnia. Any gym work was out of the question.

"I'll be lucky if I live long enough to see my Johnny fight again," he said with a groan.

Fighter Squires spent his nights sitting up and reading magazines aloud to his incapacitated pal.

Gene met the problem of his invalided trainer and non-working pugilist by stepping up his publicity about Squires. Photographs of Squires perched in a Central Park tree and knitting a pair of socks livened the sports pages.

There was one interview in which the African pugilist aroused the interest of the fight fans.

"I'm going to knock out Stribling in the third round," Squires informed the sports writers, "and I'll let you Yankees in on a secret. I learned this knockout punch from hitting my mother on the jaw every morning. She was a big woman, God rest her bones, but she was never any match for me."

These were Fowler lines memorized by fighter Squires.

Some two thousand spectators came to the Garden to see Fowler's Mother-Killer. They were, all of them, Fowler friends. A great cheer came from them when Squires entered the ring.

A few minutes later Squires squared off against Stribling. He struck a Jem Mace pose, left out, right fist cocked at his side. Fighter Squires held this pose without moving a muscle for a full minute, until Stribling banged his jaw and knocked him out. And poverty once more descended on Fowler.

SOME NEW YORK FOWLER FOOTNOTES

Gene worked on Hearst's New York *American* as an editor and reporter. He was a good editor, but what a reporter! I have no room to recite his feats, scoops, and forays; or offer samples of his crackling copy. Dean Swift, Addison, Twain, and Walt Whitman were in the Fowler "bulletin and new lead," but never crowded Fowler out of his paragraphs.

You'll have to take my word for his prowess as a reporter. I, too, had practiced journalism and delighted city and managing editors; as had MacArthur. We both took off our hats to Fowler.

Wherein lay his superior glitter as a news gatherer? Where nearly all superiority lies — in his love of living.

High officials confided in him as if he were their neighborhood priest. Defendants (kidnaper Bruno Hauptmann for example) poured their woes into his large ears. He was, by the way, large-eared as a bloodhound, and used to hope for the return of the stocking cap as a headgear that would increase his attractiveness. But he never wore one. He was too conservative.

To continue, his fellow newspapermen admired him en masse. He was never a rival, but a flattering version of their profession; and a fascinating man. A visiting Queen fell in love with him (Marie of Roumania) and had to return Fowlerless and heartbroken to her throne.

Fowler, MacArthur, and I used to sit together in speakeasies. Believe me, an audience always multiplied around us as if we were a German street band. We took long walks, going nowhere; met up with strangers, and ran into fun everywhere — although occasionally Fowler would be forced to start swinging his fists.

I witnessed a number of Fowler battles. It was never necessary to join with Fowler in a fight, and there was seldom time to do so. His fights came suddenly without preface of vocal anger, and were over almost as suddenly.

One night, having tucked MacArthur into a hotel bed, Fowler and I continued to the Friars Club where Gene had decided to do his sleeping. He was too weary to make for his Kew Gardens home.

As we neared the Friars, Fowler stumbled slightly over

some sidewalk object. A voice called, "Careful, old man, don't trip on your whiskers."

Fowler paused, turned, and saw four collegians sitting in an open car, parked near the Club. Another of the full-grown students called, "Aren't you out kind of late, Daddy?"

A third collegian (they were carrying football pennants) cried out, "Look at the poor old duffer. He sure hit that cider barrel tonight!"

Fowler moved toward the car. He grabbed the heads of two of the collegians, banging them together like a pair of cymbals. They became unconscious. He turned toward the two other fist-swinging students and dispatched each with a single blow. I had managed to cross the sidewalk to his side. Looking at the four unconscious students in the car, Fowler explained to me, "I dislike being called old."

He was in his thirties.

One of the great ones who felt the Fowler spell was W. R. Hearst, Sr. Mr. Hearst summoned him to Los Angeles for a conference. He had decided to put Fowler in as managing editor of the new Hearst paper he was creating for New York — the *Mirror*.

Fowler demurred. He felt a lack of executive blood in his arteries. But Mr. Hearst knew better.

"You are an expert in grammar and punctuation," Mr. Hearst said, "which is always a sign of high capability."

It was true about the grammar and punctuation. Fowler had a mysterious passion for proper syntax. Even in his Denver days, he regarded a misspelled word, a dangling participle, or a misplaced semicolon as disfigurements. His admirers called it his perfectionism. But it had to do with something deeper. It was a symptom of Fowler's fear of unconventionality of any sort. He dreamed of all the commas of the world in their proper places.

Much has been written about William Randolph Hearst, Sr., and much of it derogatory. I have skipped, irritably, through essays and books about him. They seemed always to be about a different Mr. Hearst than I knew casually, but knew in illuminating detail through the reports of Fowler, MacArthur, and Charles Lederer.

Lederer was Marion Davies' favorite nephew and confidant during her lifetime; and Miss Davies was Mr. Hearst's favorite lady during most of his lifetime.

From my own contacts, and from the Lederer-Fowler-MacArthur reports, I knew a Mr. Hearst who was as sprightly as a toe dancer; as merry-minded as King Cole (not Nat); as bustling as a cavalry troop coming down a hill; and as sapient and perceptive as any Grand Lama. Most of all, unbelievable though it may seem to the many Hearst biographers, the mighty journalist, to the day of his death, retained the heart of a child. He bubbled like one, played games like one, and crowed and scowled like one.

But there was no childishness in Mr. Hearst's mind, or in his copy. In his California castle at San Simeon he could have shown the red-bearded Barbarossa cards and spades on how to run an empire.

Fowler was always loyal to a boss, but he had a special attitude for Mr. Hearst.

"I've known a number of great men," Fowler said, "but Mr. Hearst is the only one I've known with greatness in him. It's something that has nothing to do with his money or power. If you stripped Mr. Hearst down to a pair of canvas pants, a sweatshirt, and a five-dollar bill, he'd stay a great man. And reappear in no time as a maharajah."

Fowler's first duty as managing editor of the forthcoming *Mirror* was to hire a staff. Of the staff he hired, he was proudest of landing the sports-page columnist, Dan Parker.

"Damon Runyon and Hype Igoe were excellent sports writers for Mr. Hearst," Fowler said thirty years later, "but Dan Parker has proved his superiority to them. He stayed alive, an important asset in any sort of writer."

On hearing that a staff was on its toes, ready to go, Mr. Hearst wired Fowler to give the new presses a trial run. He asked that a four-page sample of the *Mirror* be printed to make certain that the ink rollers and other mechanical devices were in good working order. The four sample pages required some fifteen columns of copy and a sprinkling of photographs.

Fowler took over the task. He assembled the photographs and tapped out a dozen "news stories" on his typewriter, and affixed proper headlines on them.

The stories were all about Mr. Hearst. Since the sample pages were to be seen by nobody but the printers, and were to be destroyed as soon as the presses had revealed their efficiency, Managing Editor Fowler felt that no harm lay in the copy he prepared as filler. Each of his stories related, fictitiously, a romantic conquest by Mr. Hearst with quotes from the grateful paramour concerning his extraordinary sexual powers. Mr. Hearst was as moral and unpromiscuous a man as existed in the Republic, a fact that inspired Fowler to invent the lubricious "new stories" of his boss's bedroom exploits. The stories were illustrated by photographs of nude ladies identified as Mr. Hearst's partners in his Herculean feats of venery. They were actually photographs of dropsical and bulbous nudes obtained from hospital files.

"I'm tempted to send these unfortunate ladies a copy of our sample run," said Fowler. "What an item for their scrap books! But no, we'll print five copies and destroy them as soon as we've checked."

The operators chuckled, the *Mirror* presses rolled and the five sample copies came off the nicely inked type. Fowler scanned the pages for flaws, and found none. Every story of Mr. Hearst's mythical sexual didoes and every photograph of the grateful, misshapen nudes was without blur or smudge.

Fowler tore the samples into shreds and wired Mr. Hearst: PRESSES PERFECT STOP SAMPLE RUN COMPLETE SUC- CESS STOP WE ARE READY TO ROLL STOP PLEASE ADVISE.

A startling telegram came back from Mr. Hearst, DEAR

GENE FOWLER CONGRATULATIONS STOP SAMPLE OF PRESS RUN
IS BEING FLOWN OUT TO ME STOP WILL TELEGRAPH FURTHER
INSTRUCTIONS AS SOON AS I HAVE STUDIED IT.

Fowler retired to his favorite saloon and fell to work
numbing the horror in his newspaperman's soul. After a
second bottle he telephoned Agnes, "I suggest you start
packing, and be prepared to leave the City of New York
on a half hour's notice, if possible, with our children."

"Have you resigned as managing editor?" Agnes asked.

"No, dear girl," Fowler answered, "I'll remain managing
editor until I'm decapitated. I've arranged to have my head
delivered to you in a laundry bag. Try to keep it from the
eyes of our little ones."

Fowler told me later, "I knew what had happened. I had
underestimated the cunning of genius. Mr. Hearst had arranged with one of his loyal hirelings for a sample copy to
be whisked to his Los Angeles tower."

At the end of the second day a Western Union messenger
entered the saloon in which Fowler was still sitting, and
handed him a telegram from Mr. Hearst. The message read:

DEAR GENE FOWLER HAVE CAREFULLY STUDIED YOUR FOUR
PAGE SAMPLE ISSUE OF NEW YORK MIRROR STOP CONSIDER INK
AND TYPE FACE EXCELLENT BUT EARNESTLY HOPE SUBSEQUENT
ISSUES OF THE MIRROR WILL BE LESS LIBELOUS STOP YOU MAY
START ROLLING MONDAY.

✿   ✿   ✿

Newspaperman Fowler, not yet a book writer, came for
the first time to my house in Nyack on a midnight. He
entered, mistakenly, through our greenhouse door and thus
appeared unexpectedly in my wife's (Rose's) bedroom. His
hair was rumpled. He was smoking a cigarette, and he held
one of his shoes in his hand.

"You need have no qualms about me as a house guest,"

he said. "I aways sleep with one shoe in my hand to put out any fires I may accidentally ignite."

Rose, Russian-born and with a fidelity to Russian literature that no politics could shake, said of Fowler, "He came in like Taras Bulba."

MacArthur's wife, Helen Hayes, said after meeting Fowler the first time, "From the way Charlie talked of him, I always thought Gene Fowler was a legendary figure Charlie had made up. After meeting Mr. Fowler, I realize I was only half right. He *is* a legendary figure, but Charlie didn't make him up."

The meeting had taken place in Fowler's managing editor's office of the New York *Telegraph*. During it, Fowler had gallantly addressed Helen Hayes as Miss Menken; Helen Menken was co-starring with Miss Hayes in *Mary of Scotland*. He had also disarmed an angry gambler, come to shoot the editor for some misstatements about him in the paper. Fowler removed the indignant reader's .45 from his hand with a judo chop, while continuing his social talk with the MacArthurs — "By God, Charles, you never told me your wife, Miss Menken, was not only a genius but a woman of staggering beauty."

Fowler's first dip into literature was the writing of a biography he called, *Madam Silk*. It recounted the ups and downs of Mattie Silk, a leading whorehouse madam of Denver in the time of Fowler's adolescence. He brought the manuscript to Nyack for Charlie and me to read. We were charmed by the bawdy and hilarious adventures of Denver's "Nana." After we had done praising the book, Fowler said:

"I don't think I'll try to get it published. It might give people a wrong impression."

MacArthur argued against Gene's stand. I, also, spoke against it. After listening to our attacks on him as a yellow belly, Fowler said:

"I don't want to enter the literary world as an expert on

whorehouses. I haven't seen or talked to a whore for fifteen years. At least, not knowingly. But the critics would be sure to figure I had taken a few hours off from pimping to write it. A decidedly wrong impression."

As far as I know, *Madam Silk* is still unpublished. Fowler's knowledge of bawds as well as his intimate knowledge of prize fighters, wrestlers, thieves, con men, and killers is not to be found in his books. It was not fear of "a wrong impression," only, that kept them from his pages. Involved also was a curious modesty, a masculine distaste for bragging of masculinity. He was at the other end of the spectrum from the he-man Hemingway rushing his tourist's information into print.

After writing (and having published) some novels more respectable than *Madam Silk*, Fowler started on a biography of New York lawyer William J. Fallon, to be called *The Great Mouthpiece*. And he was finally at home as a writer. He was able to write of someone other than himself. With Fowler out of the way, the Fowler pen grew a wing or two; his phrases began to roar, his sentences to zoom.

Fowler brought me sections of his Fallon book to read and criticize. Each section had some ten to thirty pages marked for removal. These doomed pages seemed to me each time the best writing in the manuscript. My criticism consisted of arguing Fowler into retaining the Xed-out passages.

What made him to the end of his days cut his best writing from his copy? I don't know, entirely. It had something to do with a fear of self-revelation. There is always self in any poeticized description of a street, a sky, or a fellow human being. There was also in Fowler an uncertainty as to what was good writing and what was overstatement. Not for others, but for himself.

He was baffled by the fact that writers such as Hemingway, who seemed to him a show-off with a penchant for baby talk, and Faulkner, who struck him as a muddled fellow who had picked the wrong medium in which to express himself, should be hailed as kings of their craft. But it was himself Fowler ended up doubting, not Hemingway and Faulkner.

At his work of writing, Fowler was as full of elation as a Mohammed beholding ever new heavens. Nevertheless, he had no more ego about his work when done, than a shoe clerk over a sale.

His diffidence toward literary critics was another of his ego lapses. Despite his certainty that most literary critics were in need of "physics" and fresh air, he remained always respectful toward them, and their notions about books. I never heard him denounce a critic, even when drunk; or offer private rebuttal of any sort to any derogatory comment on his work. Our touchy Gene, whose fists were always ready to fly out at any slur, sometimes bewildered me by his attitude toward sneering critics. He seemed to be on their side, and to be sincerely wishful of apologizing to them for having not done well. We called this "the Fowler back-bend."

I still can't tell if it was his way of hiding the smarts of criticism, or part of a natural humility, such as induces sinners to kiss the rod. It is difficult to understand virtues missing in oneself. I could only stare at them in Fowler.

As a reward for keeping him from cutting the bursts of fine writing out of *The Great Mouthpiece*, Fowler dedicated the book to me; an honor I still enjoy.

❂ ❂ ❂

Late one hot summer evening Fowler stood naked in the bathroom of his Algonquin Hotel suite, where he had holed up to do some writing. He was brushing his teeth and gargling before retiring. The glass of gargle water slipped out of his hand, shattered on the washbasin, and its sharp pieces gored his exposed member. No other inch of him was wounded.

Stunned by this inexplicable assault on his manhood — as curious a piece of bad luck as ever befell a mentule — Fowler, spurting blood like a geyser, summoned his friend Dr. Sam Hirshfeld on the phone. By the time Sam arrived with needle and thread, Fowler, consciousness ebbing, was sitting in a room full of gore. Dr. Hirshfeld revived his muttering, embittered patient, and repaired the lacerated phallus with a number of baseball seams.

I was wandering around the town that night and decided to have a chat with Fowler before going home to Nyack. I found a white-faced Gene and a perspiring Sam.

"It's unique among accidents," I agreed, after hearing its details.

"It's the work of some envious poltergeist," said Fowler. I suggested hospitalization.

"No," said Fowler, "I'd rather not have nurses puttering around me at this time. Or nosy visitors wanting to know the nature of my ailment. They'd be bound to go away with wrong impressions. Why don't I go to Nyack with you and we can write that play we've talked about?"

We wrote the play in Nyack, *The Great Magoo*, with results almost as drastic as that produced by the broken gargle glass. The drama critics greeted our play like a lynching mob. It was strung up chiefly for being too lewd a tale for the Broadway stage. As Gene would say were he still around, we were over-restless and ahead of our time. Our merry drama today would sound no lewder than a Handel Oratorio.

On the second night of its "run," three husky fellows appeared backstage. They wished to talk to our producer, Billy Rose.

Fowler, Mr. Rose, and I listened to the visitors in a closed dressing room, a room in which history was almost made. The three huskies were muscle men from an underworld organization that had helped finance the production of *The Great Magoo*. (Magoo, by the way, means a female sexpot.)

Our visitors wished to know which three of the nine anti-Magoo critics Mr. Rose would prefer to have bumped off.

"Just give us the names of the ones you think are the worst guilty. And you don't have to worry. When we go out of here, we never saw you, and you never saw us."

Mr. Rose asked the visitors to remain seated and spoke out firmly against the massacre of Percy Hammond, Burns Mantle, Alexander Woollcott, or any of their fellow fault finders. The three visitors listened glumly, departed; and *The Great Magoo* was off the boards in a week, with no lives lost.

Fowler spoke coolly of Mr. Rose, thereafter.

"Of course, Mr. Rose did the right thing, but he is definitely not a man to have in your corner."

Fowler's response to the critics' mugging we had undergone surprised me. He was fearful of critics but, apparently, it was a curious kind of fear; for they seemed unable to hurt him.

I have known sturdy spirited playwrights to take to their beds after an adverse verdict from our newspaper drama critics; to sob hysterically for days; to threaten suicide behind locked bathroom doors; to leave New York in a rage; even to migrate, bag and baggage, to some foreign, more amiable land.

None of these reactions was Fowler's. He seemed only to bloom in the shower of brickbats. He read out loud each of the critic blasts at our play, and laughed with genuine amusement — over something. I couldn't quite figure out what, except that he seemed like a hardy mariner enjoying a good storm. Or, perhaps, a man enjoying a stroll around a hotel on a tenth-story window ledge.

MacArthur used to say when the critics rapped one of our joint works, "We're not going to answer back. Answering back is only showing your wounds."

Fowler had no wounds to show or hide. What, then, made him afraid of critics? I don't know. Possibly, it wasn't critics he feared. One of the rewards of a good friendship is an almost total ignorance of your friend's secrets.

I skip a hundred stories of Fowler in New York. He should have written them, himself. His damn modesty robbed American literature of a brother to Eulenspiegel, Quixote, and Ramses the Second. But a man can do no more than he does, what with the surcingles and snaffles clapped on him even in the womb.

Some years later Fowler left New York. He moved his family and all his possessions to Hollywood, California.

It was an odd departure. Our boy, Gene, with a thousand friends in the City, with a score of years spent in its vitals, left New York as a man steps out of a telephone booth. No rue was in him. He said few goodbyes. He had, seemingly, no roots to pull up.

He said to me on the phone:

"I'm glad to be getting out. I feel I have overstayed my visit."

FINALE IN LOTUS LAND

Poor Hollywood. Ebbs the celluloid life blood fast. Visitors will please not throw sticks at the Old Lady in the wheelchair. She was once Bon Bon Queen of the World, no less. Otherwise known as Babykins, the Castrator.

But let us speak no unpleasant words of her now. Let only the squeak of her wheelchair be heard. And the sighs of her faithful literati who push her through the Back Lots where her one-walled palazzos still stand.

I am reminded of an admonition from my editor long

ago. I was covering a hanging in Wheaton, Illinois — Henry Spencer was the center of attraction — when I received a message over the wire at gallows-side: PLEASE OMIT ALL GRUESOME DETAILS SMITH.

I wired Editor Henry Justin Smith back: WILL MAKE HANGING AS CHEERFUL AND OPTIMISTIC AS POSSIBLE.

So, to Fowler's last thirty years among the Hollywood Maestros who mistook their tin trumpets for Gabriel's horn. Fowler lived much of the time mid splendors; Oriental rugs, Florentine draperies, oversized sofas. Gardens bloomed outside his manor windows but he insisted on toiling in them like a day laborer. He was still building stone walls the day he died.

He made swarms of new friends, went on world tours; watched his three children mature, marry off, and turn him into a multiple grandfather. He filled his house with pets — cats, parrots, geese, dogs. And though he wore the chains of a movie writer, he continued to turn out books, some of his best ones. He wrote standing up, like a Dickensian bookkeeper.

Adventure nosed him out, but the Crusades were done. There were clamors still, but they were mostly echoes. You can find them recounted in his *Good Night, Sweet Prince, Minutes of the Last Meeting,* and other bubbling diaries.

In the big studios, Fowler wrestled his way through a score of scenarios. He could write them well if they let him alone. He was still full of boss-loyalty, but he was unable to understand their helpful suggestions, their elephantine clichés, their babykins plot turns, their cold-potato great ideas. He was unable to feed on their "genius."

The truth — Fowler was as out of place in Hollywood as a third leg on a rhumba dancer. As what man of talent isn't? Except that Fowler was unable to learn the trick of becoming untalented. If you want to scale peaks as a movie writer, you must master this trick. Clichés must come easy. Stereotypes and platitudes must spring spontaneously from your typewriter. And you must crow over them like a diamond cutter.

I seem to have betrayed my promise to make my report as cheerful and optimistic as possible. Fowler won't mind. He will chuckle in his Many Mansions. Hollywood gave him indigestion. In fact when he remarked to Agnes one afternoon that he had heartburn and would she be good enough to fetch him some baking soda, and dropped dead before the remedy arrived — I'm sure the heartburn was Hollywood, undigested; sticking in his craw, overheating his intestinal tract.

"We had been watching a ball game on television," said actor Tommy Mitchell, "and Fowler said he had to go home and do some work on that primitive stone wall he was building around his garden. Good God, it was an unexpected dying."

Mitchell is now also under the sod. It was surprising that he outlived Fowler, for he was one of Fowler's best friends. As he used to say, himself, "It's dangerous to be an intimate of Mr Fowler's. The odds are three to one on your dying, and turning into some more copy for his books. He writes excellently, but have you noted his subject matter? Dead pals, always. And I must say I don't like his constant cry, 'close ranks.'"

I'll keep my promise from here in to throw no sticks at the Old Lady in her wheel chair; to write amiably of Hollywood, and Fowler in it.

It was, in truth, an amiable place, despite its high heartburn and mortality rate. Nowhere else could talent find so many matters for assault and diatribe. And talent did not have to make its protests as did poet Bodenheim, freezing in a hall bedroom and sustaining himself on stolen liquor and discarded sandwiches. It (talent) could do its inveighing from barbecue pits, ornate rumpus rooms and, of course, those swimming pools.

Yes, our barricades were gilded. One story of gay Hollywood battle, and I'll be done with Fowler. It was his battle. I attended only as observer.

Fowler and I were collaborating on a movie script at the Metro-Goldwyn-Mayer studios in its lush days of Louis B. Mayer, Irving Thalberg, David O. Selznick, Eddie Mannix, Benny Thau, Hunt Stromberg, Bernie Hyman — all Pharaoh names in that time.

We were part of the Selznick Unit, a two-story papier-mâché building. Selznick occupied the entire lower floor, as befitted a movie producer of note. Fowler and I were shoe-horned into one of the six upper floor offices, as befitted movie writers of note. We had a sort of broom closet attached to our office in which a secretary could type up our creations.

Remembering our last collaboration, *The Great Magoo,* we approached our task warily.

"I think," said Fowler, "we ought to fix up our office first. It's a little bleak for imaginative effort."

We spent two weeks converting our writing quarters into a brothel parlor. Red velvet curtains were draped over the windows, pornographic drawings and photographs were hung on the walls. A flourishing rubber plant was placed beside the door. Black and pink laced oddments of feminine lingerie were pinned on the backs of chairs, as if discarded in a stampede to the bedrooms. We also equipped ourselves with an atomizer that held a quart of pungent perfume to be pumped hourly into our atelier.

Unaware of our décor activities, Mr. Selznick sent us a memo stating he had learned we had no secretary, which was, possibly, the reason for our not having yet produced any scenario pages. Fowler protested to Selznick on the telephone that secretaries always made him feel shy, and inhibited his literary side. But Selznick was firm. One of the M-G-M rules was that a movie writer must have a female secretary. He hoped we would not embarrass him by needless iconoclasm.

"David is a good friend and an honest man," said Fowler, "I think we should do as he requests."

Ben Piaza, head of the studio's casting office for "Extras," helped us find a secretary. Her first name was Bunny. She had won honors in a Texas beauty contest.

We borrowed a red silk ball gown from the studio's costume department. Bunny looked magnificent in it, a blond maenad with exposive contours and an open-lipped smile like a Welcome mat. We seated her in front of a typewriter, an instrument unknown to her, ordered up a dozen American Beauty roses to stand daily in a vase at her side, and instructed her in her duties.

"You will report at ten A.M. each day," said Fowler, "and bring your favorite reading matter with you. You will tell everybody who telephones us, except our wives, that we are out of the city. At 3:30 you will go to Mr. Selznick's office, ring his private door bell. When the door opens, you are to say, 'Pardon me, Mr. Selznick, Messrs. Hecht and Fowler would like to know what time it is.' Do you think you can do all that, Miss Bunny?"

"Oh, yes," said Bunny, "that's not hard at all. Would you like me to hold the bouquet of roses when I call on Mr. Selznick?"

"A good suggestion," said Fowler, "but too risky. Mr. Selznick might steal the blooms. He has a weakness for flowers."

All went well. Fowler and I sat in our bordello-ish parlor and made up a scenario. We did our own typing. Outside our door, the red ball-gowned Bunny sat dutifully reading movie magazines and frustrating scores of literati who paid her court; for no cooings could lure the faithful girl from her post. And our boss, David, obligingly gave her the correct time each afternoon.

But a battle cloud was gathering. Fowler's malarial bug made its annual arrival, and ran his temperature up a few degrees. This happened at two on the dot every afternoon.

For five years in a row before coming to Hollywood, Fowler had run a temperature, annually, of 105 to 107 degrees. He had spent a few weeks in a hospital each time and come out with more yellow and lavender spots on the backs of his hands.

Due either to the fact that his mother-in-law, Mrs. Hubbard, was a devoted Christian Scientist, or to the fact that Fowler usually hired medicos he met in saloons, his ailment had been variously diagnosed as "a state of mind," or "an intestinal kink."

I brought Dr. Sam Hirshfeld out to have a look at Fowler after his return from a fever bout in a Coney Island hospital. Fowler still felt a little languid. He fell asleep as Dr. Hirshfeld was peering into his eyeballs.

"Mr. Fowler has malaria," Sam said. And Fowler's annual brain cooking spells were, thereafter, reduced to minor discomforts such as he was experiencing in our M-G-M writer's office.

"It only lasts an hour or two, since Sam took it over," Fowler said. "There's no need to go home. But I would like to lie down while overheated."

There was no couch in our office. Inquiry of the studio's maintenance department revealed that M-G-M had a rule against placing couches in writers' offices.

"You'll have to take the matter up with Major Everest, who is in charge of studio efficiency problems," Fowler was informed.

"Thank you, sir," Fowler answered, "I'll call on Major Everest at once."

He left, and returned in an hour with a frowning face.

"Major Everest explained the situation to me," said Fowler. "It is a studio law that no writer may have a couch in his office. The major feels that at the sight of a couch in his office a writer would become overwrought with lewd thoughts and thus impair his maximum efficiency."

Fowler mopped his sweating brow.

"I have a number of important friends in the studio," he said, "but I'm not going around begging a couch off them as if I were some derelict."

"We could buy one," I suggested.

"Still a violation of the studio's no-couches-for-writers law," said Fowler. "It's the goddamnedest example of discrimination against literary men ever recorded. Every producer, director, and actor in the establishment is allowed a couch in his office on which to seduce any females he fancies, including the Seven Muses. But, by God, not writers! It makes one feel that literature was an art practiced only by black men in Alabama. Did I say literature? God forgive me, it's the fever confusing me.

"But I figured out a way of solving the situation while talking to Major Everest. I told him that unless a couch was delivered to this office by four o'clock, I would throw every stick of furniture out of the window. We have an hour in which to relax."

I remembered occasions on which Fowler had emptied hotel rooms in a like fashion, after discussion with management. It was his pattern of revolt.

Fowler stretched out with his malaria on the floor. I continued typing. The hour passed. Fowler stood up, saying he felt much cooler. He opened the larger window of our office.

And here I like to leave him, a Samson cracking the pillars of the heathen temple. One by one, our office furnishings — chairs, desks, end tables, filing cabinets and wastebaskets — went out of the window, crashing into the M-G-M studio street below.

It was a fascinating battle to watch — Fowler against the invisible forces of Hollywood that were giving him a heartburn. Bunny contributed what today is called a kafka-ish touch to the scene. She stood in the opened doorway clutching her American Beauty roses to her fine bosom, become exposed in her excitement.

Yes, we got the couch. New and better furnishings were

efficiently put in our office. No one complained. Mr. Selznick was at sea on a weekend yacht. We finished our script, *Farika, the Guest Artist*. It was never produced. And still no one complained.

Hollywood in its big days was an amiable town. It could smile tolerantly at Gene Fowler giving it battle with a barrage of furniture.

✿ ✿ ✿

October 30, 1942

My Dear Ben,

You will be amazed to know that I am writing with some difficulty but no effort — if you can unravel this paradox. Bells are ringing and the household beset by all manner of upheavals and domestic pow-wows. It is like living in the loft of a large fire house with greased poles on every hand.

I suppose you are now on chapter twelve of *Child of the Century*. That is why I make bold to bother you. An author must be bothered at all times, interrupted, harrassed and sued — as my elder son remarks shrewdly — so that his work may be sincere and well confused, both in his own mind and in the minds of his three readers.

In the hope that I can contribute something to your worriment of mind I shall ask you to send me your anecdote on the hanging of the negro who said on the gallows, in reply to whether or not he had anything to confide, "I have nothing to say at this time." I am having a chapter devoted to Barrymore at your home. In particular, I remember the night that Harry D'Arrast was present. I think I can take the liberty of putting into this chapter the events of another night, and at another of your homes, when Sadakichi and Fanny Brice did the Castle-glide. It is more convenient to write it this way and I should like to make it a dansant as well as a story of hangings. Your story would be one, and mine about the celebrated British novelist, Gilbert Frankeau, at the hanging of Chapman would be another. I would also include one that Jack saw in Mississippi. All these authentic anecdotes and happenings might well be placed in one chapter and in one locale for purposes of unity.

If you can understand any of the above statements, I should be happy to hear of it because that is the way I am writing the book — for the Seminole Indians.

I am a little confused at the moment because my granddaughter is piling up the complete works of Charles Darwin on the floor and planting her seat on Volume six, which is devoted to the Origin and History of the Dinosaur. She has just poured a weak solution of iced tea — and a warmer solution of another consonant — on Volume three, which is known as *The Cruise of the Beagle*. No, I am not drunk. It is just a general condition of paresis brought on by domestic hullaballoo.

I often have dreaded the moment when our so-called civilization arrived at that point when a man's brain is opened to the public. I had had some clairvoyant feeling that it would be exactly as it is — an exposure of stale confetti and disjointed screams.

I ask you as an old friend not to submit this letter to a psychiatrist as I want to be the last one to know that I have lost my mind.

Do you think while you are writing *Child of the Century* that you could pause between paragraphs to jot down a few things that I may have forgotten about that delightful evening, because of the fact that I was sober. It marked a return of the Barrymore mentality and charm and was followed by a sad relapse and then a steadily increasing disintegration of mind and body.

My grandchild is now editing Volume two, which is the Life and Letters of Charles Darwin. Personally I think she is right. She uses the editorial soft pencil and has brought a new note to the science of editing. She marks the paragraphs length-wise and employs the most ancient sign know to man — that of the whorl. This sign originated from one of several phenomena: the markings on sea-shells, the dust of whirl-winds, the climbing of vines, or the spiral viewed momentarily during the intercourse of swine.

But anyway, send that anecdote.

With highest personal regards,

GENE.

P.S. You can still reach me at my home because the Good Samaritan has an ambulance shortage. My grandchild is now removing the binding of a volume entitled *Affinites of Extinct Species.* She looks like one of Rubin's [Rubens'] cherubs, but in reality is an axe-murderess.

P.S. Am feeling great. Hope you are in form.

469½ South Bedford Drive
Beverly Hills, California

Dear Rose — Ben:

Fortunately for your eyes, I now have a typewriter. Even the most desperately pressed forger would not demean himself by copying my handwriting. *Almost* as bad as Ben's.

My long silence reminds me of the case of the two travelers, tight-lipped gentlemen, who sat together in a chair-car for ten hours through Kansas. They had said nothing at all during these hours. Finally one of the travelers turned to the other and exclaimed:

"You said it!"

Well, I have had more hilarious experiences than I can set down. At the present moment I am engaged in some experimental work with Leo McCarey, and if the war and its effects on the local manic depressives does not tell too mightily, I expect something to come of this alliance.

My brief contact with Mr. Zimbalist was funny. He is a splendid fellow, but it seems that when he announced to Louis B. Manure that I was being hired, that stillborn version of the Pontifex Maximus sent word that I must come hat-in-hand. I came, but it was not my hat which was being gripped. I was asked if I had any "mental reservations" concerning producers. I replied that I had reservations "not only mental, but also physical." This did not help my economic needs.

Also, it was recalled that last year, when Louis B. went to the track to put a garland of poison ivy on one of his horses — which had won by a strange break of fate and perhaps a little larceny — he was given a boo. At that time I told some of the boys that Louis had made a pardonable error. Somebody had said: "Mr. Mayer, come down and take a boo." And he had thought the word "boo" the Czechoslovakian equivalent of "bow." Another thing was quoted against me. I had said that, on calling at Metro, I had seen Irving Thalberg's shoes outside the door and that they were still empty.

Perhaps the most telling bit of evidence (all hashed up before the board of directors, sitting en banc) was a letter which I had written to a man named Saville, the producer of *Goodbye Mr. Chips*. I did not know him, but I attacked him in a personal letter for failing to give credit to one of my former co-workers, who had been driven almost to suicide by Hollywood sadists. I defended my colleague in connection with a work bought by Metro from David, entitled *Earl of Chicago*. In the letter, I told Mr. Saville not to give *me* any credit whatsoever, but to give credit to my fellow laborer or I would sprinkle nitro in his moustache. I also said that the chances were that Mr. Saville would make a good picture, and, if that were so, I might be called again to Hollywood on the strength of a credit, and that such an eventuality would give me coronary thrombosis and acute fistula.

After all these detrimental matters were brought up against your grizzled old gossip, the most profound statement of recent years fell like Mikimoto pearls from the lips of Buddha Mayer. He said, verbatim:

"I'm afraid he (Fowler) is laughing at us. Don't hire him."

In other directions, I was set to do Bill Fields and Mae West, but it so happened that the story they had was gorgonzola, and the object of the producer was to have me go on record with my friend, W.C. by telling him it was a fine yarn. This I refused to do. I withdrew rather than misguide my old elk-milking comrade, Water Closet Fields.

So now I am with McCarey. And God is love.

I keep thinking how fine it was of you, Rose and Coach Benjamin to stay in my corner during the recasting of the novel. It is a bit disquieting to recall that you did all your valiant sharpshooting at a time when you yourself were engaged in an Alamo siege of scenario writing. I am deeply grateful. Your criticisms and suggestions were marvelous, and the finished product (I hope) will please you.

I hear nothing from the East, but if you or Ben — or both — are heading this way, please send up a flare. By the way, I had dinner with Lilian Gish at Roland Young's the other night, and she is all that you have said, sweet and fine. She certainly thinks of you in glowing terms.

Is MacArthur still alive? And if so, why?

Leland called me immediately after I had begun to dicker with Zimbalist, but — need I say it — has not called me since Louis B. threw me on the spears. He (Hayward) is a bit miffed at me for saying that I would not send him any proofs of the book on the ground that the only things he can read are his palm and the TWA timetables. I expect to hear from him immediately the first bad notice is published.

Love to you both, from a Pilgrim.

GENE FOWLER

How is the play faring?

Dear Ben:

I have rushed through the job so fast that I am stuttering and chewing my own pudenda. But I want you to know that I have been thinking of my intelligent friends back where the East begins.

The boys are rather thrilled with my (fake) performance so far, and, as usual, I am amazed.

I enclose the drivel that I spoke about in my recent telegram ($5.04) and just to make you feel good, I want you to know that it provided me with a sermon-topic that was delivered with feeling at the Brown Derby at high noon.

I have acted so rabid every time your name has come up (and you certainly toppled the papier mache thrones, my lad) that there is an unwritten law here that no one even mention Hecht in Fowler's presence. I expected to be attacked for one of my remarks to an editor, which was:

"I knew you were an editor the moment I heard you speak of Hecht. An editor should have a pimp for a brother — so he'd have something to look up to."

But the editor — alas! — hath no guts. Instead of attacking me, he ass-smacks me with his labials whenever we meet.

Well, the Barrymore picture looks like a winner. I believe I shattered all speed records in getting TWO drafts out in less than eighteen days. You'll be proud of me yet. They want me to stay for another picture, and I am so God-rotted palsied with poverty that I may have to. Then the hegira. With my scrotum perfumed with moth-balls.

I am anxious to hear of your progress. Went to the fights with Dempsey last night. Lew Cody and a group of my favorite hoodlums gave me the right answers to all questions. Whenever a man wants to learn the truth, let him ask of thieves and whores. They're the only decent folk left in this welter. My best to the members of the Young Men's Success Club.

Love to Rose,

GENE

April 14, 1943

My dear Ben:

Your masonic announcement that Rosie is on the nest does not arouse the low peasant kind of humor that you may have anticipated. Quite the contrary. I am excited and enchanted. It is the greatest news I have received since my school days with Maria Theresa of the Hapsburgs. I see nothing humorous in this situation — only a great and happy portent.

The first thing that attracted my attention to Rosie some years ago was her fighting heart. I suppose I should have sat down and admired her mind, which indeed is a fine one, but that was not the case. She seemed a sort of ageless sprite, and ready to take on the champions of all branches of combat either single-handed or en masse. This quality, I am sure, will take her successfully through what the girls claim is an ordeal. She probably will romp and give with no trouble at all, and the product will be the most bouncing entity since D'Artagnan. My advice to you is to stand to one side and not get hurt because God knows you may get in the way of a fully formed and intellectual Dempsey. In other words, I am tickled to death.

Speaking of death reminds me that I also am on my back, but rise occasionally to slug it out with a gold-headed fountain pen. Among my other personal Bataans, which include my older son's divorce and my younger son's season in the Naval Hospital, I am trying to stave off our old friend Sam Hirshfeld. He has been polishing his knives and re-toothing his saws and trying to induce me to let him practise surgery. He claims I have an inflamed appendix and will not listen to me when I insist that the pain is in the region of the solar plexus instead of on the lower right side of the torso. I have at least got myself some duodenal ulcers, and have to eat baby food. (Will call on your son in due time and join him in a can of Gerbers' pulverized onions.)

What with these minor commotions of mind and belly, I have neglected writing to you. I feel that I did not comprehensively thank you for your advice on the early chapters. I told Pat about my reactions and my gratitude, and I will say this, that I combed over those chapters and eliminated much of the McGuffey's Reader information and, thanks to you, cut out an enormous amount of documentary twaddle.

I would be very happy if you could find time to thread your way once again through the rewritten parts and then take up what Pat has on hand.

Pat has been very kind about the whole thing although he is somewhat horrified at the length of the book. I am going to throw about nine hundred pages at him of which he now has three hundred and fifty. The book will be in four parts, and I am trying to deliver the first two parts by May 15. This will take our hero up to and including *Hamlet*. From then on, I go into his Hollywood decline and fall. If you see eye to eye with me on this question of length and anecdotal profligacy, perhaps you can help sell Pat on the idea that he need not worry about the length of the book or confuse it with Sandburg's *The Prairie Years*.

Your reference to Saville gave me a laugh. I once crossed wooden swords with that gentleman before I ever had met him in person. I wrote him the nastiest letter, a sort of cock-eyed epistle to the Ephesians, because he had not given credit on one of his pictures to a poor beleaguered countryman of his named Charles de Grandcourt . . .

Your letter perked me up considerably. I was amazed to learn that Dr. Harold Hyman also was bitten by the longitis bacillus. Great Christ! Has medical procedure gone as far as 1,300,000 words?

I had a letter from Harold telling me that Barrymore hated his father. He supported this conjecture with all manner of pontifical evidences so dear to the hearts of psychoanalysts who seem to be long on information and short on application.

You are quite right about these being the Golden Days of civilization, and the burying of our gold at Fort Knox is a precise symbol of what we have done with all the hard-won gold of our study, our art, and our reaching out for the humanities. I think the thing to do is not to scream or jibber about our descent into a daffy inferno, but to laugh like hell.

I was talking to W. C. Fields yesterday, and he informs me that it has taken him sixty-three years to come to the blessed point where he hates everyone and does not care a damn what happens. He assures me that this is a very comfortable state of mind. I cannot agree with him in this, and I suppose I shall remain naive until urn-time.

It is rather amusing, however, to recall our hollerings during the time of panic, a period which some originator of low labels called the "Depression," and to think of that time as having been wondrously peaceful and happy.

This would substantiate your thesis that come a year hence, or five years, we shall in retrospect think of our present bomb-ridden era of murder and international mayhem as a day spent in the Garden of the Gods.

I shall instruct the eminent Roumanian publisher to forward the first third of the book to you. I regret that it is on flimsy paper, which again may be symbolic, and I ask your eyes to forgive the imposition.

Again let me say that I am happy over your work in behalf of the census bureau. Rosie always has been athletic and active and should experience no trouble.

With the best,

GENE FOWLER

My dear Ben:

Your letters always seem to arrive like a pinch-hitter in the ninth inning. I certainly do turn a homesick eye toward the Nyack living quarters. I do not know just how I will be able to make it, but something may work out, both medically and otherwise to send me East.

Your reports on Rosie are most welcome. I gather that she is doing well and I believe she will continue to stay well, considering the great objective.

In regard to "fifty" years, it is more of a mental hazard than an actual one. I sat up all night with Willie on my fiftieth birthday anniversary, both of us looking for some sort of spectre to appear to welcome me into the ranks of senility. In fact, I stayed sober so as not to miss any nuance of the event. Nothing happened. Not one God-damned thing, and no one was more disappointed than Willie. He expected me to shrivel like the people in that daffy motion picture, *Shangre-La,* or *Lost Horizon,* — or maybe it was *Billy the Kid.*

In fact, after the first week of "fifty" I became more reliably wicked, wilder, and more reckless than I had been for the last ten years. All of this, of course, happened in my mind, but the important thing was that I believed I still could kick up my heels and butt my head against the walls of convention.

Recently, of course, and as an aftermath of motor accidents and clean living, I have been more or less a prisoner of Chillon. But if I know any of my family, and I mean the ancestors, not the contemporary relations, I shall yet make the record of Bluebeard look pale in comparison. All of these forebears were looked upon correctly as a worthless, libidinous, alcoholic, dastardly set. There was no Luther Burbank present, so far as I know, to change the seeds or bend the consequential branches after I had been planted, and sprung from the Rocky Mountain soil.

I rather think that you, at fifty, will still remain Hecht, and that is good enough for me.

Give my love to Rosie and to the anonymous supercargo. With affection,

GENE FOWLER

Dr. Sam just came in to promise to restrain his cutlery in my presence.

Dear Ben:

Your letter was one of those things that would have saved the boys in the Alamo. I remember that you once said that an author gets to the point (isolated as he is in a hotel room) where he either is buoyed up or flattened out by the psychological interruption of a word. I am so glad that you at once "get" what I am trying to do.

I don't know whether or not Pat is *really* enthused over my strange, and, as you shrewdly put it, "untimely saga." If the book is what I hope it will be, I think that he eventually will clap hands over the fact that he has on his list one item that does not smell of hand grenades and leaking aortas on the field of battle.

I am wondering one of two things: is the book so bad that Pat can't bring himself to hurt the feelings of an old and doddering pal? And/or is Pat in some sort of spiritual or physical funk ("FUNK," not the other "FU")? I wish you would make a Sherlock Holmes-Havelock Ellis survey of my friend, and advise me as to his status.

He has been splendidly polite to me — always a bad literary sign — and I most certainly am trying not to let him down. In fact, I am sitting in a kind of sublime and industrious delirium, using my guts for a Morris chair, and my flickering heart for a footstool. I remind myself of Sir Walter Scott (without his talent of course) pushing his quill with fevered fingers, Carlyle with a bellyache, and Stevenson regurgitating his bronchial tubes. Don't worry. I am in there like Harry Greb. I shall complete the task, only,

I'd like to find out if my publisher is in my corner, or has he been coppering his bets?

I sense that Pat is worried about the length. Well, you and I know that a work never is long. It may be dull, and thus earn the sobriquet of "long."

If you see eye-to-eye with me as to the worth of the book, I wish you could convince Pat that length is not a handicap. He always used to have such a remarkable, pin-wheel enthusiasm over his authors. Has the fire gone out of his fuses? Is he, perhaps, caught in some pelvic trap? Or am I kidding myself in believing that my present work is the best thing I have done? In the latter event, I shall be in one hell of a fix. I have thrown the dice on a great "fade." More than all else, I'd hate to think that I fell down on Jack. It's a kind of obsession with me, to give him a monument. Maybe I should have taken the hundred grand I've shoved aside, and spent it on a mausoleum.

I am so glad that Rosie the Nonpareil is doing so well in the training camp. The main event will find her at top form, I am sure. Please tell her for me, an old fan, to take it easy from now on, till the bell sounds. It is no disgrace to rest a bit.

I have made up a title that I like, and written a small verse from which it is taken. I shall not bother you with the verse. The title is: "THE STARLARK." With the best to all three (or four) of you.

GENE

P.S. The Baron is married now. Is in hock up to his navel. Has asthma, but keeps his spirit.

December 1, 1943

Dear Benie:

Have been exploring various deserts and other places in search of a congenial loneliness, and have been somewhat cut off from the world. Have seen no sojourners from the

East, such persons who might have some news of you and your household.

I hope that you have done your master work and I wish I could read it. My own whimsy is now in a wartime format and is poised on the launching blocks, and I hope it does not capsize when it is sent without benefit of music or domestic champagne down the waves.

Have been in the rather sulky but happy position of not going to work, although numerous letters from the bank and other interested and practical institutions have suggested that I rouse from my sublime coma and gather in a few deflated dollars.

This Fool's Paradise in which I find myself existing seems such a congenial, lazy, beach-comber's Eden that all my neuroses — well, five or six hundred of them, at least — have evaporated. How long that euphoria will persist while I am floating among the kelp of make-believe I cannot know, nor do I much care.

I like to keep in touch with my friends, however, and I might be tempted to open a letter providing the postmark is Nyack or some New York cafe in which you might be wintering.

I suppose that Jenny (known to me as "Jimmy") has survived all the scientific brutalities practised on children by that Sunday School-countenanced bastard who goes about like a complacent and beneficent Marquis De Sade sticking pins into the little children of the upper reaches of Manhattan.

I sort of fell in love with Jenny, and somehow believe she will look upon these so-called miracles of science with a cynical yet humorous disdain.

As usual, I have no news. I have an occasional communique from the business offices of the studios, and am warned periodically that to be out of work for so long a time is to be forgotten. I hope I can depend upon this. On my part most certainly I have forgotten *them.*

Give my regards to Rosie and Broadway, and tell them I won't soon be there.

With affection,

GENE FOWLER

472 North Barrington
Los Angeles (24)
California

Dear Ben:

Was happy to infer from your telegram that you are up again and at 'em (also atom).

Was unable of course to do my usual hearse chasing at the funeral of my great friend Decker. Bill Fowler served in my stead and, in fact, arranged for the funeral. It seems that John had decreed that his body be displayed among the easels at his studio. He wanted the deathbed picture of Barrymore propped up upon the casket beside the dutch-door lid of the receptacle, the upper half of which was raised. He thought this would be better composition.

The boys at the funeral parlor wanted $4,000 for the obsequies, thinking that our John died as rich as he had lived. But John of course always spent everything he made faster than he could paint — a fact which you of course know as well as anyone. Our Willy descended upon the morticians with all the wrath associated with the true journalist of other days. He hammered down the body-snatchers from four grand to $500, and then proceeded to raise the $500 among John's friends. The kid really wore himself out and was a true pal.

It seems that when John was taken ill, he was placed in a de luxe suite at the hospital, a circumstance that no one would have denied him, except that the charges were a little bit foolish, amounting to some $2,500. He had three nurses whom he abused roundly, and there were frequent resignations on the part of the shocked Florence Nightingales. Numerous suggestions to them by the dying man as to where they could place the bedpans and what they could do to themselves in general (and particular) caused complaints such as to rouse the faculty to threats of expulsion.

The ceremonies at the home included a phonograph recording, which I have not yet heard, of John's voice doing some "Cyrano." There was a spray of red roses hanging on the Barrymore deathbed sketch and, so help me, God! I am told that at the very moment the minister said, "Let us pray," this spray of flowers came down with a plop upon the unopened half of the casket lid. I remember that you once said that if anyone could come back from what is known as the Great Beyond, that Barrymore could do it. Perhaps this was some kind of a benediction, or its antithesis.

They were going to bury John in his famous red evening suit, a garment that always made him appear like a gay huntsman when rolling among the bars of our cafes roaring imprecations. But it seems that John, when making his dying plans, had asked to be buried in a darker suit, with his muffler under his chin. He did not want to be buried with his shoes on, and was not. In fact, he was not buried, but cremated.

Will says that there were mountains of flowers and some two hundred and fifty pals present, many of them weeping at the loss of a really picturesque and fine boy.

Today my son Will is out circulating again among friends of Decker, trying to induce some thirty of them to give the hospital a pint each of blood in payment in kind for the thirty transfusions given to John. He practically bankrupted the blood-bank of the Cedars of Lebanon of the certain type of blood that he had to have. Only Tony Quinn seems to have the kind of blood that matches this type, and this generous fellow—who once before supplied a quart of his blood to John in an earlier illness—seems to regard the whole matter with a look of haggard apprehension. The vast total of thirty pints staggers his imagination and makes him appear furtive at the moment.

The death of Decker has of course saddened me greatly because there are not many of his kind walking the earth now. I am beginning to feel like a survivor, alone and without my toys.

I am a little better physically, and was able to get out for ten minutes or so in the sun yesterday. I am still weak, however. Possibly the reading of thousands of pages of testimony in regard to the investigation of our late pal Jimmy Walker has delayed my recovery.

I do hope that you are rounding into form. I am sure that your condition can be corrected readily by proper diet and a bit of rest. However, I am the last person in the world to speak of rest. I seldom indulge in it.

Best regards to Rosie, and if the British approach, hang a light in the nearest Nyack church-steeple, one if by land and two if by sea, or is it the other way around? At any rate we don't want them coming through our Middle Sex village or farm. Too many nances would fall by the wayside.

Speaking of the latter phenomenon, I was told a story by Red Skelton about a nance who approached another man and invited him to what he thought to be a terrific party with liquor, sex, and a lot of other antics. The man who was invited said he was very interested in this proposal and asked: "Who else will be there?" To which the prospective host replied: "Oh, nobody. Only you and I." I leave you on this high, or degradingly low note.

With affectionate regards,

GENE FOWLER

Regards to the eminent Hippocrates, Harold the Great.
472 N. Barrington Ave.
Los Angeles 24, Calif.
June 11, 1947

March 3, 1949

Dear Ben:

Have had three days in the Mojave Desert, a holiday which for me was a long one. Am at last out of the obstetrical stirrups, and am trying to rally a few business deals to keep Sheriff Biscailuz and his winking horse away from the premises.

I got to thinking about you, and found myself looking forward to your book. A Hecht book always is a special event in my life, and has nothing to do with my long admiration of the artist. Your virtuosity has been applauded these many years, but I believe that the critics have overlooked one important thing in your successive works: that, slowly yet inexorably, there looms a fine and understanding heart, something that a great mind and a great talent kept in the shade because of intellectual stature. It is, and long has been, my conviction, that you are just at the *beginning* of your career as a writer.

As you enter the "stretch" on your memoirs, I wish you as much peace of mind as Fate allows the artist. By some fiendish paradox, the backslapping comes at the wrong time. The lonely bastard sits at his writing-board with no encouraging word. After months of expensive pain, and when one has grown ill of seeing the mauled pages, the passengers of the gravy train clamber aboard with well-meant, but ghastly flatteries. It is impolite to reply to them with a hoarse "Fuck you, Madams and Messieurs."

My best regards to you and your household.

GENE

Dear Ben:

Have just returned from San Francisco, where I stepped smack back to my foggy youth with the companionship of Tyrus Raymond Cobb, old Tom Sharkey, and numerous old timers of diamond and ring and of the press rooms of the land. There was a press club meeting which had all the grace notes of our heyday, together with the almost forgotten noises of reporters falling into spittoons, and the social attars of stale beer pools and oases of puke on battered chairs and tables. It was such a grand remnant of tradition to be found only in the gallant town by the Golden Gate, and today I feel as if it had been an old man's reverie, and I look out on this dusty Hollywoodian terrain with a feeling of deep frustration and farting kismets.

I have nothing to look forward to other than an appointment with Sam, tomorrow morning, when he will massage my bulbous prostate whilst speaking behind my back of Freud and the glandular deficiences of Hitler. I feel as if I were entirely surrounded by Brooklyn.

While holding a journalistic-athletic salon at the St. Francis up North, I ran into a nice anecdote concerning Tom Sharkey. By the way, the old warrior volunteered a poem when introduced at the Press Club — a grand, motheaten antique which stemmed from the rocking-horse-rhyme school of "The Kid's Last Fight." The fine old veteran of a hundred grisly, thumb-gouging, belly-ripping battles, attested in verse to the rewards which are always to be had "by *fighting fair*, lads." But the anecdote . . .

It seems that when old Tom was training for the first Jeffries fight, he frequented a saloon celebrated for its free lunch. He put such a dent in the lager buffet as to cause the proprietor some agony. Inasmuch as Tom was a noted figure among the fancy, and, to be sure, might one day be the champ, the owner of the saloon, not wishing to offend the great man, resorted to a ruse to discourage the sailor's gargantuan tripes. He said to his bartender:

"Take away all this free lunch for a couple of days, Al. Then get some dog biscuit. And get the hardest God damned dog biscuit there is. If you can crack it with an axe, we don't want it. Get some real hard dog biscuit. Then let's see if this Sharkey son of a bitch can go on eating us out of house and home."

The dog biscuit was laid out where the pickles, sausages, hams, and other provender used to be. Sharkey arrived after the workout, saw the biscuits, sampled one, then proceeded to eat his way through the starchy concrete pile. The next day he did the same, presumably relishing every bite. This so dumbfounded the proprietor — whose trade was beginning to lessen among those who did *not* like dog biscuit — that he told the bartender:

"Al, it's no use, for God's sake! So clean up the crumbs, see, and put back the regular lunch, see. The son of a bitch Sharkey!"

On the third day Sharkey reappeared, looked at the assortment of meats and hams. Then, after searching the free lunch bar, called out rather sharply:

"Hey, you, where in hell's them *tasties* I been getting lately?"

Appreciated the news from the East. Remember me to Rose, and to the lads at "21."

McCarey is not feeling so well. Confidentially, he is going to rest for a month or so. Meanwhile I am going to do a job, possibly, *Kitty Foyle* and then come home to write a bit on my own.

I have survived the shock well enough. A sore back is about all that bothers me, although I also have a rib which hangs in space, like a bedslat after a pimp's visitation.

With the best,

GENE.

P.S. Have been stewed but once since I enjoyed that state at your house, and on this occasion ran into Leland, and insulted him for all of us. He says he feels quite hurt and claims I didn't know what I was doing at the time.

G.

May 2, 1955

Dear Ben:

Have had no luck with the telephone to Perry Lane. Probably would have had little to say except that I can't get used to a world without "Snocker," [Snooker] even though he never really lived in the World as it is defined by the lesser mortals. From the few glimpses I had of him these last ten or twelve years, it appeared that he was a stag at bay. Everyone who runs from reality (and I have been a Wes Santee in that respect) needs "second wind" again and again. I assume that Charles used up his store of adrenalin long ago, and was track-weary.

I thought the *Time* article excellent in most respects, but cannot accept the word "voluptuous" as applied to the lad. It may have appeared to some bystanders that he indulged in sensual mechanics, (as which of us has not?) but found no genuine pleasure in such exercises. His indoctrination in evangelistic brimstones became a wall that he could not scale. I believe that he hated sex, because he feared it. Speculation?

Am back at "work." Painted my entire house and the porch furniture. The recess did me much good. Am in excellent physical condition, much to the amazement of the medical men. As to my mind, I never was afflicted in that respect by too much intellect. Hence, I have little to lose.

Speaking of doctors, I have a problem: Harold Hyman's ms. of his novel is here. Justine sent it to me for comment. I am, in any event, a miserably incompetent critic! I am unable to see the difference between a toy balloon and a cannon-ball. Harold's book seems to lack organization, character, development; is burdened with too many chapter-headings that do not have chapters; and he tells three or four stories in competition with one another. I don't know

what to do or say about this, for when it comes to my so-
called profession and the practice of it, I simply cannot tell
a lie. What in hell can I do? Harold is such a wonderful
man, and his fiction is not in keeping with his genius. Love
to Rosie and Miss Jenny. And to you my perennial affection.

GENE

About Mencken

There are novelists, playwrights, poets today as rampant as any yesterday. Indeed, more so, since the police department censors have taken their noses out of the arts.

But there is no successor for H. L. Mencken. Put together the ten most whooping critics of our current American scene and you won't have the beginnings of a Mencken. The Sage of Baltimore is gone from our midst, and his boots remain empty.

To any reader past fifty, a briefing on Mencken is hardly necessary. If he and she are reading me today it is likely they read Mencken yesterday, and remember with a grin his all-out campaigns against the Babbitts, the Bible Belt, and the Booboisie. But the land is overrun with young people, bright and sassy ones, to whom the nearest of yesterdays are as dim as the Stone Age.

True, there are no statues of Mencken around to bear me out, no monuments or memorial plaques. Nevertheless, H. L. Mencken was the mightiest verbal warrior of our century. He was a one-man war against the U.S.A. He launched his hostilities around 1910 and kept them going, vigorously, for twenty years.

He edited a magazine called *The Smart Set,* which is like calling Cape Kennedy "Lovers' Lane." And he wrote hundreds of essays and scores of books beginning with a series more informatively titled, "Prejudices." But the verb "wrote" doesn't give a right picture of his product. He exploded books and essays. It was hard to believe that one man could make so much noise and mow down so many Idols, Icons, and Sacred Cows.

My last sentence is rather misleading. It suggests scenes of great public excitement. There were no such scenes to note. At the height of his rampaging, very few people were aware of the goings on. Like most intellectual forces, Mencken fought chiefly in a vacuum, and with the grandstands almost empty. His broadsides attracted about as much attention as if he were sitting on the moon, shying stones into space.

H. L. Mencken's war aims, according to the handful of observers who deigned to notice his conflict, were the overthrow of American Democracy, the Christian religion, and the YMCA. He was also credited with trying to wipe out poets and luncheon orators.

But these were unfriendly as well as shallow versions of what Mencken was up to. I knew Mencken from the time I was seventeen, and though I was hardly more informed than a monkey in a tree, I understood H. L. Mencken thoroughly in that time; and my understanding never changed.

Mencken was an uplifter, an evangelical battler for the soul of man. He hoped to help along the process of human evolution by revealing what dunces people still were. He once said to me:

"Have you ever watched a crab on the shore crawling backward in search of the Atlantic Ocean, and missing it? That's the way the mind of man operates."

Mencken went after the backwardness of human reason, idea by idea, myth by myth, pomposity by pomposity. His assaults appeared originally in the back pages of *The Smart Set*. I considered the magazine with its delicate blue cover a sort of monthly Gospel. As far as I was concerned there was no other critic or philosopher in the land. Only Mencken. I believed everything he wrote, and rejoiced over his destruction of all human sham and flapdoodle.

I was a little upset in my 'teens that hardly anybody seemed to be paying any attention to the fact that H. L. Mencken was making over the world. His name was not to be heard in the saloons and press rooms I frequented as a budding journalist. Nor was it to be spotted in the nation's book pages or literary magazines.

Yet I was certain that Mencken was a greater influence in the Republic than both its Houses of Congress. He *was* reshaping American thought, whether anybody cared to notice it or not. There was a Mencken underground, not only of writers who cribbed his attitudes, but of university professors, statesmen, and bachelor girls. And young newspapermen like myself.

As I said at the start, Mencken is not much read today, no more than Tom Paine, Walt Whitman, James Gibbons Huneker, Percival Pollard, Ambrose Bierce, or William James. Mencken is a museum piece, an old brass cannon behind a red velvet rope.

I may be wrong. H. L. Mencken may still be sustaining an underground with his fulminations. If so, it's a pussyfooting underground that mutters into its sleeve about political and religious buncombe and the assininity of the human species. I don't know why vigor went out of the American mind, and why a con-man blandness replaced it. It may have something to do with atomic explosions having put a blanket on intellectual ones. And something to do with the fact that in Mencken's day the fear of Communism hadn't throttled free thinking — not in Russia (who gives a damn about Russia?) but in the U.S.A.

SOME GIDDY HOURS WITH MENCKEN

I was eighteen when I met Mencken. He was covering the 1912 Republican National Convention in Chicago for the Baltimore *Sun*. The convention was held in the Coliseum, an enormous wooden structure on the near South Side. I had been entrusted by my city editor to gather some "Sidelights on the Convention." "Sidelights" meant any kind of odd little stories you could make up out of whole cloth and attach to some national figure.

I recognized Mencken from a rare photograph of him I had bought for ten cents in a book store. He was in his thirties but he didn't look young. He had a round face that had reminded me even in the photograph of a City Alderman. It seemed even less intellectual in life. He was around five feet, nine inches in height. Sitting in the blistering hot hall with his coat off, he looked like a man who had never played a physical game of any sort. He was not fat or ill shapen but seemingly without muscles. His waistline bulged, his shoulders hunched; he mopped his face with slow gestures.

I sat down beside Mencken in the press section, as beside Socrates, Aristotle, Voltaire, and Nietzsche. He knew my name, for he had printed two short stories I had sent him, and had written me a number of letters on his blue-tinted, half-sized stationery. In that day Mencken's letters descended like manna on scores of land-locked literary Jasons. The first glints of talent in a manuscript fetched friendly salutes from this fiercest of critics. I used to save and reread his letters and show them around as if they were citations. They were, for several years, the only letters I received that weren't sent me by my mother. I wish I had all of them for this book, but some fifty changes of residence have gutted my treasures.

But I remember the letters. Many of them offered me brief plots for further stories, such as the following. "Write a story," read a letter from Mencken, "about a young Mormon in Utah who falls so deeply in love with a young woman that he refuses to wed and take into his bed the three more wives prescribed by the Mormon Gospel of that time. And so he flees with his one wife and lives in sinful monogomy with her, in St. Louis."

I wrote the story and he gratefully added ten dollars to his editorial check, raising my take to forty-five dollars per story.

In another letter Mencken wrote, "Try a story about a Polish immigrant who works in the Chicago stock yards as a ten-dollar-a-week pig sticker, and who practices fiddle playing all night. So does the Mr. Swift who owns the stock yards and lives in a millionaire's mansion. Mr. Swift, the millionaire, is consumed with ambition to be a great fiddle player. And for an ending have millionaire Swift sitting in his box in Orchestra Hall, listening with searing envy to a great new fiddle player — the same ten-dollar-a-week pig sticking Polack who worked for him."

Mencken printed this one under the title "Humoresque in Ham," and added another five dollars to my author's check.

I wrote dozens of stories for Mencken later. He never rejected one, an understandable approval considering the convict prices he paid for fiction. He was pleased also by the fact that I didn't mind his signing pseudonyms to my stories. This enabled him to run two or three of them in a single issue. There was also the fact, to please him, that even if my stories were my own plots they still read as if a sort of snorting, amateur Mencken had written them.

In the Coliseum that scorcher of a July morning, I was too excited sitting beside Mencken to notice that the man I considered the most important brain of our time was without acquaintances, let alone admirers, in the big convention hall. He seemed to know everybody and informed me of their political status and intellectual caliber, but no one seemed to know him. At least I had no competition for his company.

"There's a gentleman you probably esteemed as a child," Mencken said. He pointed to the front row of the press section where sat a good-looking man in khaki shorts, a pith helmet, and binoculars slung from his shoulder.

"That's Richard Harding Davis," said Mencken, "he dresses more entertainingly than he writes." Then Mencken smiled and added, "You liked his Van Bibber stories and Captain Macklin and so weiter. Don't worry, I won't hold it against you. I am, myself, a graduate of 'Nick Carter' and 'Fred Fearnot.'"

*   *   *

A year later I visited Mencken in his Baltimore home. He had invited me — "If you ever come eastward drop in on a Wednesday evening around seven. I'm always home on Wednesdays. And be sure and bring your fiddle."

On my next vacation from the paper, I bankrupted myself buying railroad tickets to New York, Baltimore, and return. I arrived at Mencken's house at 7 P.M. on a Wednesday.

It was almost as hot as it had been in the Chicago Convention Hall. Mencken, again in shirt sleeves, opened the front door. He seemed to be alone in the large wooden house, whose magic address was printed on his stationery.

We went into a room almost obliterated by books. Mencken sat down at an upright piano. He offered me a bottle of beer. I accepted it politely, without saying I never drank beer. No glass came with it. I drank out of the bottle. There was no mention, despite the hour, of food.

"You're a little early," Mencken said, "the boys will be here in a half hour or so."

"You said seven o'clock, Mr. Mencken," I reminded him.

"Call me Menck," he answered, "and never take me literally."

"I know," I said, "Nietzsche wrote 'he who would follow me must first forget me.'"

Mencken hit a few chords, "No literature tonight. Music. Schumann, Mozart. We may even try Beethoven. God love 'em all."

He told me, then, that the boys who were coming were three members of the Baltimore Symphony Orchestra. They came on Wednesday evenings to play quartets, with Mencken at the piano.

"You will make a fifth," he said. He handed me some second violin parts of Schumann and Mozart, and suggested I look them over while he warmed up.

As I studied the music pages, Mencken began to play. I thought at first the room was equipped with some special sound amplifiers. But there was no such artifice involved. Mencken played the piano as if it were a bass drum. With his foot pinning the loud pedal to the floor, he banged out a Cèsar Franck piece louder than any piano solo I had ever heard.

I changed my mind about his being a man without muscles. His forearms, hands, and fingers were obviously as powerful as a blackmith's.

He went on playing like a man under a spell. I grew dizzy listening to the piano tumult and, possibly, also from hunger.

At nine o'clock no symphony musicians had showed up. I noted another item. The telephone had not rung. In his home town, I had as little competition for his company as in Chicago.

I felt saddened by my hero's lack of popularity. I had always imagined that his days and nights were so crowded with admirers clamoring to see him that it was a wonder he found time to write anything. While he played, I noticed three letters on his large, flat-topped desk. One of them was from me.

I felt an insight into Mencken. This revolutionist assailing the human mind, this battler in a hundred worlds of thought, was a lonely man. He lived in a room heaped with books and made a loud noise on his piano.

"Get tuned up, we'll try a duet." Mencken stopped playing. "Have another beer first." He handed me one. "I guess the boys aren't coming. Too hot a night for them. Musicians are delicate fellows. Except, of course, opera singers who are all hardy as boilermakers, and as disturbing to the ear."

I had read Mencken on opera singers and nodded. How talk to a man whose every opinion on every subject you knew verbatim?

We played several duets together. My fiddling was no match for his piano accompaniment. It was like playing a duet with a riveter. I yelled at him to pipe down so I could hear my own strings. He considered this a confession of defeat.

"Pretty hard stuff," he said, "but I think with a little practice you could play it."

"I can play it now," I said, "except I can't hear it, the way you beat the hell out of that piano. Do you want to try Schubert's *Unfinished?*"

I rosined my bow and stepped to the other side of the room. We played the *Unfinished Symphony* through, and ended nicely at the same time.

A sweat-soaked and exhausted Mencken stretched out on a couch.

"You're in no hurry to leave, are you?" he asked. It was only half-past nine. I said I was in no hurry.

"I'd like to talk to you," said Mencken. "You remind me of an event in my life. The way you sit there looking at me is how I once sat in a Baltimore hotel room looking at a writer named Percival Pollard. I held him to be the greatest American critic alive. I was somewhat wrong, as we all are when we're nineteen and pick out our great Pooh-Bahs to admire. How old are you?"

"I'm going to be nineteen," I said, "but haven't picked wrong."

"Could be you're different," said Mencken. I refrained from saying, "You're different from Pollard." Instead I tried to remember what Mencken had written of his own eating habits. It seemed impossible that a man who had worked so hard at the piano would go without food all evening.

"Pollard wrote one good book," said Mencken, *"Masks and Minstrels of New Germany.* His other stuff aged badly. However when he came to Baltimore, he was the nation's finest critic in my eyes. In fact, he came here because of a number of adulatory letters I had written to him in San Francisco. My God, Pollard had known Bierce, London, Sterling, Morrow, and all the first-rate Westerners. And he had met up in Germany with Frank Wedekind and Otto Julius Bierbaum."

I'll tell the rest of Mencken's story in my own words. Its points are still vivid in my head, but Menck's voice and phrases have dimmed.

Mencken's literary idol, Percival Pollard, arrived in Baltimore on a freezing December day. The great Western critic was in flight from his wife who had offered him harassments beyond endurance.

Pollard was also down to a hundred-dollar bank roll but, he assured his young disciple, Mencken, the money was sufficient to see him through to his finish. The doctors had told him he was in the last stages of tuberculosis and would not live the year out.

Mencken induced his literary hero to enter a hospital.

"It's a foolish waste of money," Pollard said, enfevered in a hospital bed. "Much cheaper to die in a hotel room."

Mencken visited Pollard daily. At the end of a week Pollard said to his disciple, "I think I'll be gone in the morning. And I would like to ask one favor of you, a last favor."

Pollard had a distaste for coffins and cadavers. He wished to be cremated instead of buried. Mencken gave his idol his word of honor to see to the cremation of his body.

"One more request," said Pollard, "there is only one

human being in the world who cherishes me a bit — my aunt in Waterloo, Iowa. Will you send her my ashes to inter in any way she sees fit?"

Mencken promised this would also be done. Pollard was dead in a few days. Young Mencken managed to find a crematorium in Baltimore. It was a primitive institution, consisting of a bed of coals kept red hot by several forges. Percival Pollard's remains required six days to incinerate.

"I used to go out every day," said Mencken, "and try to hurry them up at the forges."

On the seventh day, Mencken was finally given a tin box containing Pollard's ashes. He wrapped the box properly, addressed it to the aunt in Waterloo, Iowa, and hurried to the post office. Here he made a slight blunder. He tried to insure the package to Walterloo.

"What does it contain?" asked the postmaster.

"The ashes of America's finest critic," said Mencken.

"You can't send human remains in any form through the mail," Mencken was informed. "You have to accompany the deceased in person to his destination."

And the young Mencken was warned against trying to violate the postal laws. Federal punishment was always swift and certain. Even daring crooks hesitated to stir government sleuths into action.

"I remembered a speech in a melodrama," said Mencken, "made by an unfortunate character as the irons were clapped on his wrists, 'Don't monkey with Uncle Sam. Twenty years is a long, long time.' To this day I still cower at the sight of a letter carrier."

Frightened from the mailbox, Mencken considered traveling to Iowa with the great critic's ashes legally in his pocket. But he decided first to call on a friend of great influence in the city. The friend was head bartender of Baltimore's finest saloon — a bailiwick teeming with national statesmen.

On hearing the story, the bartender assured Mencken he could handle the problem. He would pull a few political strings and Mr. Pollard's ashes could be dispatched to Iowa without expensive escort.

I remember Mencken's finale of the story.

"I waited patiently and asked no questions," said Mencken, "until I received a letter from Pollard's aunt in Waterloo. She was overflowing with gratitude for my having sent her the ashes of her beloved nephew. She had buried him in the family graveyard, next to her own mother, and had ordered a stone shaft to be properly inscribed and placed over his remains.

"I hurried to thank my bartender friend for having fulfilled my mission for me. I asked him what politician had helped, so that I might return the favor sometime.

"My bartender friend blushed and told me he had tried a half-dozen politicians and had been turned down by all of them. Nobody wanted to have his finger in a violation of the Federal postal laws.

"And my friend had then taken the matter into his own hands. He had thrown away the tin box with Pollard's ashes in it. Instead he had bought a box of Cremo cigars, and wrapped the box impressively with layers of tin foil. And sent it on to the aunt in Waterloo.

"So today, under a tombstone proclaiming that here lies a great man of letters, Percival Pollard, rests a box of disintegrating Cremo cigars, which should warn you of the dangers of becoming a literary man. There is no telling how you may end up."

I left Mencken's house around midnight, lightheaded with hunger, but full of great spiritual sustenance. And I did not change as he did toward his cigar-bewitched hero. Mencken is still Mencken to me.

"THE ARISTOCRAT AMONG MAGAZINES"

Telephone: Bryant 4895   *25 West 45th Street*
New York

THE SMART SET
A Magazine of Cleverness

GEORGE JEAN NATHAN ⎫
and   ⎬   *Editors*
H. L. MENCKEN ⎭

Dear Ben:

It is a refined and stimulating idea. I shall bring the merits of V. Baden to the notice of the local intelligentsia.

Hay-fever has me by the coccyx. Let me have your progress.

Thanks for steering MacArthur this way. His hanging story thrills me.

MENCKEN

THE SMART SET
Printing Crafts Bldg.
34th Street and 8th Ave.
New York
April 16th

Dear Hecht:

Don't let anyone set you to doing what you don't want to do. You have a sound technical equipment and can afford to experiment. This thing here seems to me a bit Poeish and strained — some of the episodes in "Grimaces" were much better, particularly the police court scene — but choose your own poison, and go on with it. Nathan is laid up by bad eyes and can't read. If you ever feel like sending any of the other things I'll be glad to read them.

In Baltimore several policemen were converted by Billy Sunday. Perhaps this may suggest a buffoonish tale to you. The other cops refused to speak to them. In the end they got into such rows that they were exiled to the most remote posts — far-flung steppes beyond the city dump. Or have them locked up as crazy.

Yours in Xt.,
H. L. MENCKEN

1524 Hollins Street
Baltimore, Md.

June 26th

Dear Hecht:

You deserve no credit for penetrating Nathan's disguise. A blind orphan might have done it. The man is sentimental to the verge of oleaginousness.

Do not forget the Greenwich Village complex: art with a capital T, not F.

I trust you proceed assiduously with your literary endeavors. We need copy,

In Xt.,

M

H. L. Mencken
1524 Hollins St.
Baltimore.

January 15, 1943

Dear Ben:

The other day I was going through some old *Smart Set* correspondence and found a number of letters from you, *circa* 1917. They were full of plans for a book, to be called "Grimaces." What was this book, and did you ever publish it? I can't identify it, but it occurs to me that you may have brought it out under some other name.

I seize the opportunity to hope that you are in good

health and full of wayward thoughts. As for me, I gradually oxidize, but nevertheless the medical brethren report that I am still alive.

Yours,

M

H. L. Mencken
1524 Hollins St.
Baltimore

January 29, 1943

Dear Ben:

Your tribute to my virtues really touches me. I needn't tell you that I agree with you secretly, though I am forced, of course, to dissent in public.

God knows it is a long time since our last session. When ordinarily, are you in New York? Let me know and we can arrange for a meeting. I propose sitting down to lunch together. I have a plan for a book of my own that I want to explain to you, and maybe I'll ask you for a few facts. I am now approaching 63, and begin to realize that if I am ever to get my record on paper at all I must hump myself.

I still stop at the Algonquin when I am in Gomorrah, so there should be no difficulty about fixing the time and place for a session. I'll probably be in New York again about the middle of February.

Yours,

M

H. L. Mencken
1524 Hollins St.
Baltimore.

June 8, 1943

Dear Ben:

I surely hope that your sweatings for humanity have not put out of your mind altogether that brief account of yourself for my record. Some day when the mood is on you lock yourself up with your beautiful secretary and dictate a column or so of names and dates.

I am constantly reminded of the Chinese saying: It is later than you think. You are still in the full tide of vigor and sin, but I begin to realize sadly that the years that have passed are gone forever. If in these gloomy days I drink as much as four seidel of beer I begin to feel full. It is a dreadful sensation.

Yours,

M

H. L. Mencken
1524 Hollins St.
Baltimore

June 17, 1943

Dear Ben:

The news that you are to become a father at your advanced age is news indeed. Please give my best wishes to Mrs. Hecht. Tell her that my chaplain is instructed to pray for her and the baby. I'd add you also, but I am convinced that prayers would do you no good.

Please don't burden yourself with that record. What I want is an account of your life that is a little better than the one in "Who's Who," — that is, I want to know where you spent your boyhood, how you got on a newspaper, and what your early adventures were as a literary gent. Where and when did you print your first story? If you want to hold this saga into 1,000 words, very good, but if you choose to run it on to 300,000, so much the better. I want to add it to the record of my days as editor — probably not to be published until after I am an angel.

Yours,

M

About Sherwood Anderson

You couldn't tell whether Sherwood was lying or telling the truth when he spoke of himself. He seemed to be lying, but why should a man lie about being a cruel and deceitful fellow, if he wasn't? To make himself fascinating? If you knew Sherwood you would smile at that answer. Our cornfield Balzac-to-be had no more interest in what you thought of him than in the responses of a June bug.

His surprising revelations in his talk were not part of any need to lie, or to impress people. He talked of himself like a man strumming a mandolin. The strumming was not for listeners. He liked to hear stories about himself. I don't know if he talked about himself out loud when he was alone. But that's what he seemed to be doing when others were around.

The first stories I heard from Sherwood were of his pre-Chicago days. He said he had been born in the Ozark Mountains, and had lived his boyhood among moonshiners and illiterates. That's where they had dubbed him "Swatty," due to his belligerent nature. That part of the story didn't sound convincing. The Sherwood of thirty-three was no more belligerent than a mole.

"I came to Ohio," said Sherwood, "and I got to be head man of a big factory in this Ohio town. All the people of the town bought stock in my factory. They sort of co-owned it with me and they were all pretty sure I was going to make them rich.

"The factory caught fire one morning and burned down into a pile of ashes. And the townspeople stood watching the factory burn down, and take all their money with it. Not caring to listen to the wailing of any co-owners of the factory, I just wandered off into the cornfields and pretended I had lost my memory and didn't even know my own name.

"I grew a beard and wandered around for three weeks. People saw me and reported that I'd gone crazy. And they felt sorrier for me than for themselves. Some of them came after me in the cornfield and tried to talk me back into being sane. But I just wiggled my beard at them, and pretended not to know who they were or who I was."

"What happened then?" I asked.

"Well" — Sherwood's outstretched arm waved a hand gently in the air as if he were hypnotizing an unseen listener — "well, they finally toted me back home. I was too weak from starving to resist them. And a lovely woman nursed me — my wife, Cornelia. And my young sons gathered around my bed, wishing me well. But I decided I'd had enough of all of them. Particularly my lovely wife, Cornelia. She'd been a schoolteacher, and she'd taught me to read books. But she got to insisting that I read the wrong ones, books without secrets in them. I didn't like the further schooling she had to offer, so I left them all.

"And here I am, a happy man making a good living and waiting for people to wake up and recognize me as the best writer in America."

I believed, as much as did Sherwood, that this was bound to happen. I had sat in his Cass Street room with a half-dozen others and listened to him read from his frequently rejected and as yet unpublished manuscripts, *Windy Mc-Pherson's Son, Marching Men,* and *Winesburg, Ohio.*

The writing held us but it was the voice that sold us its greatness. Sherwood read his writings like a preacher offering revelations.

He was in many ways like a preacher who had found God. The God was himself.

Sherwood was an attractive-looking man in his thirties. He seemed to have too much hair on his head; and also too many features. This was because there was too much expression in his face. The odd thing was that this most sensitive of men I knew, never tried to please anybody. He considered it everybody's duty to please him.

One evening, sitting on the lake front, he told me of a girl named Fedya. He was, obviously, going a little out of his way to educate me. He thought that I was "a newspaper Ned" blind to the truths of life, but "not too stupid for talking to."

"Fedya loved me very much," said Sherwood. "I told her in bed one night, 'it's unwise for a man to let a woman love him too much. It's like his over-borrowing at a bank. He has to pay it all back, in some way or other. Paying back is always a big strain.'

"When I woke up in the morning, Fedya and all her trappings were gone. I felt strong with a feeling of relief. A man always feels relieved when it stops raining kisses."

Sherwood's words still singsong in my ear. I have forgotten the way he wrote, but not the way he spoke.

I had seen Fedya and Sherwood together. She used to sit on the floor with her head against his knee as he read from some newly rejected manuscript. She was a thin, tense, and dreamy-faced girl with her blond hair cut in a bob, an unusual hair-do for those days. Most girls carried a yard or more of hair on their heads in pompadours, braids, and buns.

One evening, in Amy Fancher's studio on the South Side, Sherwood said:

"I received a letter today and a small news clipping from a friend of Fedya's in California. Fedya was living in a place called Laguna Beach. She bought a white horse to ride. The other day she rode her white horse off a cliff and fell on the rocks fifty feet below, and was killed."

Sherwood's voice was calm. He spoke of Fedya's death as if he had gotten rid of a rival for his affections. He now had the field to himself.

Except there was Amy Fancher. That wasn't her name. I

prefer to spare her shade the unpleasantness of reading her true name linked again with Sherwood. She didn't ride off on any white horse, but she tried to.

We were all young; I in my teens; Amy and Sherwood, the oldest among us, in their early thirties. There seemed to be no elderly Chicagoans. There was young Michael Carmichael Carr, in his black cape with a silver buckle holding it closed at his neck. He had come from Italy where he had been working as Gordon Craig's associate. They had been sawing out puppets and were going to have puppets take the place of actors in the theatres of the world. The project was Craig's, possibly because he was striking back at his mother. He was the illegitimate son of the famed English actress, Ellen Terry.

There was young Alexander Kazi, a cultured bomb thrower from St. Petersburg, Russia. He was Sasha, our Nihilist. Later he became professor of Russian literature at the University of California in Berkeley. But now, still young, he was busy seducing Chicago girls by singing melancholy Russian songs to them.

Sherwood tried to keep Sasha out of his Cass Street soirées — "Stay away from me, Sasha. I got no time for foreign fakers."

Sasha, who could have dropped him with a single poke, only nodded his head and looked full of sympathy. Sherwood explained to me,

"The Russians [he called them Rooshians] have no sense of honor. They'll come into your home, uninvited, eat your food, drink your liquor, and try to steal your girl."

This was true about Sasha, the future university professor. He stole nearly everybody's girl, including one that poet Bodenheim loved madly. Her name was Valerie. She was a blonde beauty, and a self-supporting commercial artist. Sasha married her. One evening when he had become a university professor at Berkeley, Sasha was driving through the California woods with a pretty co-ed at his side. When the car came to a halt in a darkened glen, its trunk door opened and Valerie stepped out and took a few shots at her husband. One of them hit him and Professor Kazi was laid up for a time. There was scandal around his name, but when he returned to his pedagogical duties, his classes in Russian literature were larger than ever.

Of Sherwood, our Russian menace said:

"The world will some day recognize him as a fine writer. But for me he will remain always an inch high beside Turgeniev and Andreyev."

Sasha later wrote books about his literary heroes, without putting Sherwood's name in them.

There were around Sherwood in those days Bodenheim, MacArthur, Floyd Dell, Vachel Lindsay, Edgar Lee Masters, Carl Sandburg, Alfred Kreymborg, Eunice Tietjens, Cloyd Head, Jerome Franck, Margaret Anderson, Harriet Monroe, Jane Heap, Henry Sell, Sam Putnam, Harry Hansen, Burton Rascoe, Llewellyn Jones, Clarence Darrow, Stanislaus Szukalski, and Jerry Blum, back from the South Seas with a load of paintings and a touch of mania that landed him in the crazy house at Dunning, Illinois.

Nearly all of these, and others like them, were better known than Sherwood. But they were, nevertheless, part of his court. Sherwood, who had never had a line of writing printed except advertising slogans done for his firm, was the great one in our fermenting town.

We were a windy lot, given to bragging and denouncing our successful elders, particularly if they were writers of books. But Sherwood went us one better. He denounced *us*, not with anger but with a chuckle. We were, he said, without anybody hitting him in the nose, a parcel of crude and noisy "would-be's." We would never come close to the secrets of life, among which he, himself, sat enthroned.

Young J. P. McEvoy said of Sherwood:

"He could become a millionaire if he had anything but hot air to sell."

In later years I understood the superiority that Sherwood flaunted over us. We were all buzzing with ego, and full of plans to capture the world. But none of us was full of the magic of self-love. It is a potent quality for any sort of artist to have — from strip-teaser to sonneteer. Love yourself, and others will come eagerly to your side to compete with you. Self-love is a potent advertisement of your desirability.

People were drawn to the wonders Sherwood saw in himself, as to a riches to be shared. And there they came a-cropper. Sherwood had no nuggets to give away. The only outsiders he could love were the characters his pencil created. And these were not outsiders, they were all Sherwoods. He crooned over them and sang like a poet of their big and little troubles.

Despite the aura of self that was his homeland, Sherwood was a likable man. He had the charm of indifference. The world was run by unimportant strangers, trying vainly to attract Sherwood's eye with a lot of meaningless events. I don't remember his ever mentioning World War I while it was going on, even after he came back from his first visit to Paris in 1917. He talked then only of James Joyce, Gertie Stein, Picasso, George Antheil, Modigliani, and other artistic people.

"They're my sort of people," Sherwood said, "they like me. They treated me respectfully as if I was a whole cornfield, a sort of force of nature."

The battles of the Marne and Verdun had no place in Sherwood's tales of wartime Paris.

Sherwood's indifference to critics was as genuine as his indifference to wars. He said of most literary critics, "They'll come around to me sometime, but that won't mean they've gotten any smarter. All such critics are interested in is stealing a ride on somebody's bandwagon. They have no transportation of their own."

When Sherwood's great success came to him, he remained the same as he had been in his years of rejections. He lived outside of other people's adulation as he had lived outside their indifference. Fame added no strut to him. He still concentrated on loving himself, and to Hell with the rest of the planet.

What makes such a man likable? I try to remember, and finally do. His talent. You felt his talent all the time you were near him. It was like being conscious of a beautiful woman's beauty.

It made you understand and condone his self-love. There was something remarkable in him for him to love. He had a way of talking and writing that was different than anyone else's. He echoed no one. He was something freshly hatched. He was Modernism — the unwanted orphan on the doorstep of complacency.

Sherwood knew he was a Modernist. The knowledge made him more complacent even than his Tory enemies who had no use for his "morbidity," "decadence," "immoral hog wash."

As a Modernist, Sherwood Anderson finally heard the noise of fame around him for a time. Thomas Wolfe said of Anderson, "He was the only man in America who ever taught me anything."

Sinclair Lewis said, "Sherwood should have received the Nobel Prize instead of me."

As Sherwood had forecast, many critics boarded his bandwagon, and proved what refined intellects they were by tooting their horns for Sherwood Anderson.

But, suddenly, where there had been practically no bandwagons for high-class critics to jump on, the Republic became full of them. And the critics took to deserting one for the other, thus making fame fitful and dubious.

Sherwood's fame dimmed even while he was alive. After he died in 1941, his readers seemed to die with him.

It was the thing that often happens to literary talent that is a touch too modern. It becomes old hat a little more quickly than the talent that is less odd.

TALE OF A PSYCHOLOGIST AT PLAY

I used to envy Sherwood his girls, or rather the way he won their devotion. He did no noticeable courting, wasted no time (or money) on them, and had no aftermath problems. Unless you wish to call Fedya hurling herself to death off a California cliff a problem. Sherwood did not regard it as such.

All Sherwood did to win the love of maiden or matron was declare himself available. It was like putting up a bargain sale sign.

Amy Fancher was Sherwood's longest lasting unmarital romance. Amy was his mistress for a year. She was a divorcée, aged thirty-two. Her husband was a successful novelist who had wandered off in quest of more exciting females.

Amy was a homely woman with a freckled, round face. She dressed in plain clothes, wore low-heeled shoes, and hairpins were always falling out of the braids on top of her head. She looked shapeless. She wore rimless glasses. Her face, in summer as well as winter, looked frost-bitten.

But Amy was everything inside that was missing in her exterior. She was a woman of high spirit, quick wit, and sensitivity. She was full of poetry, old and new; and loved books as if they were all Bibles. And her nature was as emotional and sensual as any Isolde or Heloise. She was also self-supporting, and a generous hostess.

Although "living in sin" was still socially incorrect in those days, no one ever criticized Amy's romance. Her love for Sherwood was delightful to see and hear. She gave parties for him, took charge of readdressing and mailing off again his rejected manuscripts. She asked nothing of him, never nagged, never turned a jealous look on his Yogi gurglings at younger, fairer girls.

And Sherwood beamed on her love and spent weeks living in her studio.

"We sat up all last night," Amy said, "and Sherwood talked about the secrets of people. It was so wonderful. It was like hearing a god talk. Sherwood is almost that— he's a great artist."

Thus the romance went until one autumn day when a girl telephoned me at my newspaper. She was Amy's best friend. They had rented a small house in a Chicago suburb and were living in it together. It was a rainy morning, and the girl on the phone said:

"I'm terribly worried about Amy. She left our cabin about two hours ago. She walked out into the rain without a coat or umbrella. And she hasn't come back."

The girl asked me to come out to the suburban town and help her look for Amy.

"Amy," she said, "is in a terrible state. She's absolutely heartbroken. She bought some poison last week. I found the bottle and emptied it."

I walked in the pelting autumn rain with Amy's friend. I said I was sure Amy was too sensible a woman to commit suicide over Sherwood no matter what he'd done. She had always said, "A man can't love unless he feels free." And she had offered other such remarks that made her seem the finest type of woman, if only she were a bit more appealing to the eye.

After an hour's plodding in the rain, we came on Amy. She was sitting on the edge of a railroad embankment. She

had emptied a bottle of liquor and she was waiting drunkenly for a next train to come along and run her over.

In the cabin, Amy told her story. Sherwood had refused
to see her or speak to her on the phone. He had returned
her letters unopened. And there was no reason for his behavior. She would have let him go had he asked her. There
had been no quarrel. He had just pushed her out of his
life after a year of love and friendship, without explanation.
If he had told her he didn't love her any more, or that he
had found another girl, Amy would have patted his cheek
and let him go without tears or complaint. Sherwood knew
that. So why did he suddenly slam every door in her face,
without saying a word. It was this mystery that was horrid
and made her want to die.

I promised Amy to find out from Sherwood why he had
removed himself so abruptly from her.

Sherwood said at our cafe table, "I'll tell you why I've
broken off with Amy. And you can pass it on to her, if
you so wish."

He spoke as if he were handing down a judgment rather
than making a confession. He said he had decided delib-
erately a year ago to become Amy's lover because he
wanted to find out at firsthand what it was like to live and
cohabit with a woman whose homeliness repelled you sex-
ually. And who was so generally unattractive from any
sensual point of view that she made you wish you were a
eunuch.

"The worst side of the affair," said Sherwood, "was having to keep on lying to Amy. Having to say all those lying
'I love yous,' and 'I want yous.' They really take it out of a
man. Make up some excuse to Amy now? Why should I?
She's had a year of me, much too long. And I'm sick and
tired of lying to her. I knew I couldn't tell her another lie,
if I started a farewell scene. I'd tell her what I've told you.
And I just didn't care to go that far — as a psychologist."

I lied for Sherwood. I told Amy that he had become

infatuated with a seventeen-year-old chorus girl and was too ashamed of what he was doing to face Amy.

"He begged me to tell you the whole truth," I said. "He said that when his stupid infatuation wears off he'll be able to see you and talk to you and he hopes you'll forgive him."

Amy was happy. She smiled and "understood" as they say in Bohemia. Sherwood was a great artist, a man of superhuman sensitivities. When I saw Sherwood again would I tell him she would be proud all her life to have shared a year of it with him.

I would never have told Amy's story, even though Amy is dead, if she hadn't known it already. Some five years after her affair with Sherwood, he wrote her a long letter from Paris in which he explained his psychological experiment—his amour with a homely, undesirable woman; Amy —"I always admired you but I wanted to find out what it was like to hate somebody you'd admired, as a result of having to pretend you loved the person—as is the case in nearly all marriages."

Now that Amy knew the truth about their affair, would she care to write him what her feelings were about him? He was working on a book called *Many Marriages,* and Amy's attitude toward the truth—"the secret truth of our relationship," might be helpful to his book.

"I would like to write him," said Amy, "but I don't know what to say to him. I've forgotten our old affair. I can't even remember our nights together, except the ones when he talked. Dear Sherwood, he did talk beautifully."

I imagine Sherwood must have told this story in Paris, at least to his young disciple, Ernest Hemingway. Sherwood was the model for a number of Hemingway's male heroes, lording it over the girls in print.

But Hemingway, after proclaiming his indebtedness to Sherwood, was among the vanguard that started to turn on our great one, as soon as his greatness began to get in the way. Hemingway wrote a book, *The Torrents of Spring*, in which he burlesqued Sherwood Anderson's style, and tried to reveal Sherwood's phoniness as a writer.

It didn't help Sherwood, but it didn't unhorse him.

"I don't have to hit him back," said Sherwood, "Ernest is such a shut-in, fathead sort of writer that he's going to end up burlesquing himself. And he'll do it a lot better than I could."

AN ADIOS

I hadn't seen Sherwood Anderson for some thirteen years when I came into "Jack and Charlie's" New York cafe one winter's night in 1941. He was sitting with a new critical conquest, George Jean Nathan. I joined the pair.

Sherwood was heavier, and the too many features of his face included a pelican pouch chin. His hair was still black (with dye) and not a curl of it gone.

But there was a change in his voice. It had become an imitation of the Sherwood voice I remembered well. It was louder and its water-whistle laughter seemed fakey. The old superiority singsong was missing.

After we had exchanged insults and belittling memories for an hour (for Nathan's benefit), I said good night. But Sherwood put a hand on my arm and kept me in my chair a few minutes longer.

"I'm going away," Sherwood smiled. "That ought to make an item for your newspaper writing."

It did. I was doing a daily column for the underdog-championing newspaper *PM*. I wrote of the hail and farewell meeting in the cafe, as follows:

"I'm leaving," Sherwood said. "I'm going to Santiago, Chile, by boat."

How long would he be gone?

"Oh, pretty long," said Sherwood. "Maybe a year. Maybe two. Maybe forever."

Why was he going?

"I don't know," said Sherwood, "you write why I'm going. If anybody ought to know about me, it's you. Write what you want."

I wrote in my newspaper column,

"I ought to know and do. Sherwood is off to find something that vanished out of the world he knew and wrote about. It disappeared out of the land. It was the American he knew — that moody, whimsical, inarticulate hero of the pre-radio, pre-movie hinterlands. Something scotched him. And Sherwood, his great biographer, is off for strange lands, where he can forget his hero is dead."

A *PM* copy boy dropped a news wire on my desk as I finished reading my story about Sherwood in *PM* print. The news wire reported that Sherwood Anderson had just died on the ship nearing its South American port.

He had been in the ship's bar eating some before-dinner tidbits. And he had swallowed a small sausage with a toothpick still stuck in it. The toothpick had perforated an organ and killed him.

Cornelia Anderson, Sherwood's divorced wife, wrote me the following letter, after his death:

227 *East Tenth St.*
Michigan City, Ind.

March 17, 1941

Dear Ben Hecht,

I want to thank you for your splendid tribute to Sherwood. It was a masterpiece of understanding. What a pity he could not have seen it.

Embarking upon a new adventure would seem a perfect way for him to die, if only it weren't for the long trip home.

They leave Panama the eighteenth and the burial will be at Marion, March 26.

I almost subscribe to the belief that the spirit must restlessly flit about the Styx until the sacred rites have been performed.

Thank you again for the fine appreciation and its title.

Sincerely yours,

CORNELIA LANE ANDERSON

[I had called the piece "Go-Scholar Gypsy."]

Ben

I am going on the west side about 10 in the morning and will be back about 2 P.M. At 3.30 I have an apointment with a man in the Straus Bldg. at Clark & Madison. I'll be through there at 4.30. Where will you be between 4.30 & 5 P.M. Call me at the office in the morning and tell me. Call before 9. Wabash 3146.

SHERWOOD

Your letter expresses the whole matter of cours[e].

Ben.

Last night I lit into that satire on the matter we talked of. Had three men in a saloon, a tall grey haired man from a country town, a red faced man who lived in Evanston and belonged to a lodge and the bartender. It was delicious but after I had got into bed I got up and tore the thing to bits.

The truth is Ben that from my point of view it's interference and I can't do it. You have got to take into consideration the constant illness through which this child has passed. I myself have seen her almost choked to death and to go almost all night without sleep is a not uncommon experience with her.

How do we know that all of these mannerisms that sometimes make us impatient are but defences set up by a spirit that is often at the breaking point. Let's forget it all Ben old boy.

It's a hell of a job for a woman to get through life. There are men like you and me, more or less sensitive, pretty clean, rather skillful in arousing affection. We want women of a certain kind and in a blundering sort of way we try to create them out of the material that presents itself to us. We forget ourselves and forget the hungry, sometimes unruly passion asleep in the woman. That's in us too but it's different. Can you really now conceive of yourself as living your life for women.

Well think it over. This woman, of whom we talked, has done that more than you imagine. She is doing it now, doing it and being defeated. Also she has been defeated in health. She half wanted to write and that didn't go. She has a madness for a certain kind of social power and she has had to see her influence over Floyd, Mike, you and me wane. Let's let it rest, Ben. Dammit man it isn't in the cards.

SHERWOOD

My Dear Ben.

I am going to answer your letter by insulting you. I have carried it 2 days and have not read it until now proped up in the lower berth of a sleeper at Davenport Iowa.

Well I should say your lack of selectiveness is apparent in your letter. Out of your own mouth I condemn you. 7 dozen shreds of ideas and none of them developed relentlessly, given form. My mind has to go forward and piece together the bundles of words. You have taken bits out of the midst of thoughts and flung them at me without stopping to think that as used they have neither beginning or ending.

You spring the Mike idea in regard to the lady's knee. A nice example. Mike absorbed in the lady's knees. Me absorbed in Mike. He got the knees, I got Mike, the knee, and Mike's lovely appreciation of the knee.

It's a matter of style, dear Ben, style in living. You and Mike can take the knees. I will be putting in that time finding the combination of knees, lips, white teeth, fine eyes, clear voice — oh all that — not so rare if you haven't your eye glued on a knee.

Your picture of the idea of selection being carried to the hermit's den is dramatic but not true. As a matter of fact life gives you what you ask of it.

For example you speak of becoming religious as a thing to be dreamed of. Where is my poet. While you have been talking I have done it. Yesterday in the midst of office hours I twice burst into tears because of a new conception of the man Jesus that had come to me.

Begone and quit defending yourself. Yours is the attitude of the minor poet jumping back and forth about a subject. Suppose you do miss some of the beauty spots along the road. Is there nothing to be said for the journey's end. Are all writers to loiter forever. Be up and away. Put away the playthings. Age comes on. Life is short. Get the style in life that is due to economy in spending yourself on the minor. A[t]tack the loafer.

SHERWOOD

Dear Ben,

This sounds much more reasonable and crooked and altogether healthy and OK, you should however bludgeon a rich man or woman into giving you and Sell a bunch of money in the name of art and avoid the sweat and other vulgar manifestations of labor. A man who has been working smells so. A year ago I tried to get a gang of high class yeggmen to take up this project but they preferred to rob henroosts instead. I got some pickpockets to try it but they were common bubs and mussed it up. One of them was to approach Mr Myerbloomgreenbaum — or whats the hells his name of Sears Roebuck and Co and engage him in earnest conversation regarding how the air of Chicago had already produced you Sandburg and me and as time went on would probably produce worse.

As tears flowed down the cheeks of the mail order party a fair faced lad disguised as Jane Heap was to take the roll out of his rear pants pocket. The scheme would probably have gone through as Rose Searsbuck was on the point of hysterics but Burton Rascoe tipped it off because you were in it. Fear of arrest really accounts for my sudden flight to these parts.

I'm for anything crooked but like to be approached as a fellow crook.

I'll say this — with old Hank Sell in the gang I'd undertake to make a living raising doves.

You let art alone. She's got enough guys sleeping with her.

SHERWOOD SUREFIRE.

I'm not much scared yet!

About Bodenheim

Maxwell Bodenheim was more disliked, derided, denounced, beaten up, and kicked down more flights of stairs than any poet of whom I have ever heard or read. He was also more ignored than any literary talent of his time.

His seven volumes of poetry fetched him hardly a thimbleful of notice. Not acclaim, but ordinary notice such as is given the most inconsequential bores who darken the lives of literary critics.

Yes, my friend Bogie whose work I admired more than the poetry of most of his famed contemporaries was a total washout as a literary contender. His glowing metaphors seemed to remain invisible to the critics. And without critics to give a poet a leg-up, he is likely to remain in limbo. No lecture dates, no college faculty jobs, no royalty checks. And, of course, no invitations to the White House or other important showcases for the poetry writer.

But I doubt whether poet Bodenheim ever daydreamed of such grand finales. From the time I first met him in his Chicago teens, Bogie had a mystic sense of himself as an unwanted one. No one asked him for lunch or dinner. He was a sort of unharnessed human. You watched him scampering around, and never thought of offering him shelter or the diversion of friendship. Besides, you knew what happened if you did — insults, rows, thefts, and complaints from the neighbors.

It wasn't true. Bogie was often a guest in my home. He revealed a few oddities that stood my teeth on edge. But I preferred him to the usual visitors, who droned through card games, or put me to sleep with political discussions.

Another truth was Bogie's attitude toward social invitations. It pleased him immensely to turn them down. "Thank you for inviting me to dine at your house," he wrote a well-to-do lady who fancied she was running a salon, "but I prefer to dine in the Greek restaurant at Wabash Avenue and 12th Street where I will be limited to finding dead flies in my soup."

Of his rapidly growing unpopularity in his youth, poet Bodenheim said, with a mocking grin:

"Nobody seems to like me. Do you think it is because I am too aware of people's tiny hearts and massive stupidities?"

"They are too aware of your big mouth," I told him. "Why don't you try ignoring their imperfections, after sundown?"

"I was born without your talent for bootlicking," said my friend Bogie. He crowed with delight and whacked his thigh.

Despite the continuing, unvarying defeats of his life, it is this strut I remember as Bogie's signature. Ignored, slapped around, reduced to beggary, Bodenheim's mocking grin remained flying in his private global war like a tattered flag. God knows what he was mocking. Possibly, mankind.

I may be writing of a Bodenheim with a special routine in my presence. He may have whined and wept elsewhere. But not the Bodenheim I knew. Disaster was never able to disarm him. Even the Greenwich Village moocher, half-starved and ragged, remained proud of his ability "to destroy people on my guillotine of phrases. Oh, boy, stick around and you'll see some heads roll."

It was not Sherwood's sort of self-love that kept Bogie abloom. It was his incredible sense of superiority. In his last years, tottering drunkenly to sleep on flophouse floors, shabby and gaunt as any Bowery bum, Bogie hugged his undiminished riches — his poet's vocabulary and his genius for winning arguments. He won nothing else.

New York, after 1924, failed to alter him by a hair. He wrote of New York, "the poverty of its ash cans cannot match the pathetic debris in the heads of its literary critics."

Nearly everyone who met Bodenheim was either irritated or outraged by him; and frequently moved to take a swing at his nose. Although poet Bodenheim had small ability as a pugilist, it was unwise to attack him physically. He threw things. Bottles, chairs, vases, plates, carafes, end tables, started flying across the room. Such missiles always belonged to some aggrieved host or hostess who had not even invited him. Bodenheim, in his lifetime, never owned a cup or saucer to aid him in combat.

The poet also alienated rafts of people who had never met him, but "had heard of him." They heard that on a dance floor poet Bodenheim was certain to cut in, enfold your wife or sweetheart in a lecherous grip, and insist that she go to bed with him, pronto.

I never witnessed the spectacle of Bogie trying to drag a dancing partner into the hay, and ending never in a bed, but hurtling headfirst out of a doorway. There may have been a grain or two of truth in such gossip, for the poet wrote, in our *Chicago Literary Times:*

"Since the dubious dawn of human history, dancing has been one of the more adroit female ruses for the sexual stimulation of the male. A young woman who embraces a man while he is being assailed by primitive drum beats and bacchanalian horn tootings, may pretend she is interested only in the technique of dancing. I wonder if the same young woman, naked in bed with a man, would insist that she is only testing out the mattress."

Another rumor had it that the poet arrived at studio parties carrying a burlap bag into which he transferred speedily all the canapés and liquor bottles available. I could verify this rumor, and also another one — to come within earshot of the poet was to be derided stridently for any convictions you had about anything.

These tales were to be heard in Bodenheim's heyday, his twenties and thirties, before he had matured into a Greenwich Village sot. He became, then, too pathetic a fellow to punch in the nose or kick down the stairs.

Only the police continued to beat him up, due to his defiance as a Communist orator. He would not climb down a ladder from which he had been addressing a noon-hour audience of factory workers, or cease his oratory.

The truth is that Bogie was the sort of Communist who would have been booted out of Moscow, overnight. He insisted that Communism was a cure-all for the miseries of the poor. Stalin and his selfless colleagues were toiling to create a Utopia of peace on earth and good will to men.

"How can you be against the Russian politicians, as you call them," asked my friend, "when those alleged politicians are doing exactly what Jesus Christ tried to do — eliminate war and tyranny from the life of mankind? Russia," he smiled happily, "has rediscovered love and justice, and is ready to turn the other cheek to the capitalistic bullies of the world. Yes, siree, Moscow is the new Mount of Olives."

Bogie dreamed that in Stalin's Russia he would find all the good meals and sensitive understanding that he had been denied in the U.S. Lacking carfare to go have a look at his cornucopia land, he aired his fondness for it — with the usual Bodenheim results. He not only angered the police but disturbed, equally, the Communist Party leaders of New York. They denounced Bodenheim as a nuisance and refused to print his proletarian poems, gratis, in their red periodicals.

*   *   *

Why did a young man as talented as Max Bodenheim bring such a load of bricks down on his head, until the day he had it, literally, blown off by a crazy man's gun? I'll tell a few Bodenheim stories that may partly answer the query. Bodenheim was in his youth a slim fellow with blond hair, albino eyebrows over pale eyes, five feet ten inches in height. He had a lean, handsome face, and all his teeth. His clothes were shabby but clean, and included in winter an American army overcoat. He had joined the U.S. forces at seventeen and been stationed a year in Texas, half of that time in the regimental guardhouse. He had been put behind bars for hitting a lieutenant over the head with his musket. The lieutenant had been ridiculing Private Bodenheim as a Jew.

Bogie carried all his worldly belongings with him. They were in the bulging brief case held under his right arm. In this case were all his unpublished poems, an extra pair of socks and underpants, a spare tin of tobacco for his corncob pipe, rejection slips from the nation's editors and a bottle of tobasco sauce.

RARE ITEM—A BOGIE VALENTINE

Bodenheim journeyed to New York as the salaried Eastern correspondent for a weekly paper I had started called *The Chicago Literary Times*. He received thirty dollars a week for his Gotham reports, and his name was on the paper's masthead as assistant editor. I filled some seventy per cent of the paper with copy, Bogie wrote most of the remaining thirty per cent. There were a few intruders, among them Lloyd Lewis, Vincent Starrett, Wallace Smith, Rose Caylor, George Grosz, Herman Rosse, Stanislaus Szukalski. I wrote in the paper of my editorial assistant:

"Maxwell Bodenheim, in manner and appearance, is the ideal lunatic. He is somewhat bow-legged and possessed of malicious, pale green eyes one associates with murderers.

"While engaged in arguments (he has seemingly nothing

else to do) Bodenheim improvises brilliantly. He accompanies his razor edged epigrams with startling grimaces. He bares his teeth in sudden snorts. He clucks unexpectedly with his tongue, as if summoning a flock of chickens to enjoy his wit. He beats a tattoo with his right foot, and whacks triumphantly at his thigh.

"Excited by the withering fire-power of his phrases, he starts bobbing his head like a pigeon on a trail of popcorn. During rebuttal by an opponent, he gives vent to cat-calls and ear splitting guffaws.

"The expressions of his face are usually unrelated to his subject matter. While hamstringing a critic (and he can) he adopts a pensive look—

"'H. L. Mencken suffers from the hallucination that he is H. L. Mencken. There is no cure for a disease of that magnitude.'

"During such utterances, he flutters his yellow fringed eyelids, cocks his head to a side and pretends he is falling asleep. His grimaces remind me of a child making faces out of ennui.

"Yet despite the chronic ferocity of his opinions, Bodenheim is a sentimental man. Anyone's sufferings but his own bring a tear to his eye or pencil. He gives away most of his wealth—nickles and dimes acquired in alley crap games—to beggers, old drunks and cigar butt hunters.

"Behind his almost idiotic guffaws and facial contortions, a first-rate mind is in constant operation. H. L. Mencken, who despises him, cannot assail his 'dunderheads' as wittily as can Bodenheim. Despite the hallucinations of grandeur and nightmares of persecution that bother Bodenheim, the poet retains an astonishing diagnostic clarity toward others.

"Bodenheim's poetry and prose are a worship, chiefly, of words.

"I have known Bodenheim to be mistaken by casual observers for a pickpocket, a vaudeville acrobat, an errand boy, a theological student and a French aristocrat."

What I wrote of Bodenheim in 1924 was true but it over-looked almost entirely the poet's charms. There was in-nocence and courage in him, and wild loyalty. And his misfortunes seldom produced a note of self-pity.

TALES OF A CUBISTIC NIGHTINGALE

We collaborated during one winter on several one-act plays. One of them was called *The Master Poisoner.* We were both excited in its writing. We thought it contained our finest acrobatic phrases. When I read the play recently, I was astonished by its plot and dialogue. They were both incomprehensible. Yet the printed phrases seemed to spin and leap with some mysterious excitement. Youth in love with words. The embrace may have been a little disorderly, but I have found few things better to love — since then.

We worked nights. Bogie would arrive at my apartment at eight o'clock, having filched his supper elsewhere. I didn't invite him to dine in my house because I hated to watch him eat. My wife also found the spectacle unpleasant. He drank like a man gargling, and wolfed his food as if he feared it might be snatched away.

But his table noises were a minor matter. It was *what* he ate that was upsetting. As soon as his food was placed be-fore him, Bogie set up a clamor for Worcestershire sauce. He emptied a full bottle on his steak or chicken. He then fished his bottle of tobasco sauce out of his brief case and sprinkled the fiery fluid over his food. For a finale, he un-screwed the tops of all the salt and pepper shakers on the table and coated his sauce-drenched food with their con-tents. A jackal would have shied from his dish.

As important to collaboration as not watching Bogie eat,

was not hearing his denunciations of his enemies, who seemed to have overrun the world. We made a pact that during our writing together, neither of us would utter a word of criticism or complaint on any subject.

Bogie was a half hour late one evening. A blizzard had delayed him. He entered the room with the remains of a pipe clutched in his teeth. It had been a pipe brought back from the South Seas by the painter Jerry Bloom. It was a pipe four feet long and its carved bowl rested on your foot as you stood smoking it. Jerry had given Bodenheim the pipe (the only one like it in the Western Hemisphere) in exchange for a sonnet by the poet describing one of his seascapes.

"The streetcar step was covered with frozen snow when I alighted from it," Bogie explained. "I was smoking the pipe at the time, and tripped over it and it broke into little pieces." The yellow eyelashes fluttered. "Shall we start with our collaborating for tonight?"

We worked till midnight. I noted an oddity in Bogie's posture. He kept his head in a crooked position as he offered his share of our weird dialogue. He made no complaint, however, of any injury; and I thought it wiser not to inquire if anything was the matter with him.

At midnight Bogie bowed himself out of my doorway. "I think we have done some exquisitely confusing work tonight," he said, "we will resume our capricious wrestling match with Mr. Maldor, tomorrow, same time." Mr. Maldor was our Master Poisoner.

We didn't resume the next night. After leaving my apartment Bodenheim collapsed in a snowdrift. An ambulance took him to the County Hospital. I learned the next day that Bogie had broken his shoulder when he had tripped over his Polynesian pipe. He had spent the three hours writing with me while in acute pain. But he had honored our collaborator pact — no complaints.

OF A LAVENDER BALLERINA

During the winter of our playwriting, Bodenheim was in love with a dancing girl named Ilona. She had been a member of the Chicago Grand Opera ballet troupe, but was dismissed that season from its ranks.

"Due to the insensate jealousy of Signorina Pitalli, the première danseuse," Bodenheim explained. "Beside Ilona, Miss Pitalli became aware that she was glued to the stage."

"That is partly true," Ilona said. We were together in an all-night beanery. The ousted ballerina was mostly skin and bones. But I remember her large, glittering eyes, favorably. They hinted at some mania. She informed Bogie that she was going to be given an audition by a vaudeville booking agent named Sam Singer. She had been working on a wonderful dance that she called "Lavender and Old Lace."

"I've got the costume for it," she said, "except for the shoes. I need a pair of lavender ballet slippers. And I guarantee you, Maxy dearest, I'll bowl Sam Singer over with my routine."

A great quarrel developed between the lovers. Bogie forbade his Ilona to go near Sam Singer. I left the table while the poet and Ilona were exchanging violent insults.

I didn't see Bogie again for several weeks. I remember that he sat with me in a saloon one night, tears running from his eyes:

"We kept on quarreling for two days about Sam Singer," said Bogie. "Then we separated. I told her she could go dance for Mr. Sam Singer in her tights, but in doing so, she was dancing out of my life, forever. Last night I realized that I was crude and unjust to Ilona. I decided to go to her and apologize for my ugliness, and beg her to forgive me.

When I arrived at her rooming house, the landlady told me that Miss Ilona Metz had died five days ago of pneumonia and that she was now in her grave in the Woodlawn Cemetery. Can you loan me ten dollars, please, so that I can buy Ilona the lavender dancing shoes she wished for. I want to put them at the foot of her grave."

The next night, Bogie told me the end of the story. It has stayed in my mind ever since as a sort of ballet in which a poet dances the strange, secret meanings of his life.

After leaving me with the ten dollars in his pocket, he had dropped into another saloon for a drink. A prostitute joined him, there. He bought her a drink and then read a newly written poem to the prostitute. It was about Ilona's dying and titled "Elegy to a Pirouette." After reading his complete cycle of Ilona poems to the prostitute, he went with her to her room.

"When I woke this morning," Bogie said, "she was still asleep. I dressed quickly. Then I looked in my brief case which should have contained the eight dollars remaining from the original ten. I intended to give the prostitute two dollars and then go buy the lavender dancing slippers for Ilona. But there wasn't a single simoleon in the brief case. I knew at once that I had been robbed after I fell asleep. I knew also it would be a pure waste of time to accuse her of the theft, or to try to get back my stolen money. She would start yelling and policemen would ultimately appear and take us both off to jail.

"Then I felt an electric shock as I noticed something on the floor — the sleeping prostitute's shoes. They were purple shoes with purple buttons on them. They were not shoes for dancing, but they had a gay look of their own."

Bodenheim stole the sleeping prostitute's shoes and a few hours later placed them at the foot of Ilona's grave.

"Exposure to wind and snow," he explained, "will fade their purple color to the right shade of lavender that Ilona wished for to match her costume. I wrote this poem to Ilona while riding in the streetcar."

Bogie recited a poem of which I remember a few lines:

Dancer on the floor of heaven,
These once industrious shoes
Now dream of you.

TALES OF MARTYRDOM, LAUGHTER, AND URINATION

News came to us that the young poet Maxwell Bodenheim had refused to register for military service in the First World War. He had announced himself as a conscientious objector. A number of radicals in the Near North Side had undertaken to protect him from military oppression. They had hidden him away in a lush apartment, and were providing him with excellent food and drink; and allowing a trusty trollop to spend a night, now and then, with him.

A few of us who knew the Federal Building as newspaper reporters, called on the proper authorities to persuade them to stop hounding our sensitive poet and causing him to remain in hiding, a-tremble for his life.

"You're a bunch of fools," the head recruiting officer told us, "your poet friend Bodenheim registered for service on the first day our office opened. Here's his card. Nobody's hunting for him. Your friend is ineligible for further Army service. He was dishonorably discharged after previous Army service in Texas. The United States Army has no interest in him whatsoever except to keep the daffy sonofabitch out of its ranks."

This news finally leaked out to the radicals who were win-ing and dining their heroic conscientious objector in the flossy apartment. Loud with wrath, they descended on the poet. They excoriated him as a crook and a charlatan, and drove him out of his sybaritic hideaway.

Listening pensively to the rage of his deceived benefactors, Bodenheim fluttered his eyelids and announced, "The anger of fools is my favorite crown."

*   *   *

Bodenheim came to dinner in my house, having promised to forego sauce bottles and salt and pepper shakers. It was a party of welcome to a new writer for *The Chicago Literary Times*. Its staff to date had remained only Bodenheim and I. I thought it time to add another worker.

His name was John Armstrong. He had sent me the manuscript of a novel written while in detention at the Great Lakes Naval Training Station at Lake Forest. It was a fascinating manuscript, detailing the miseries and frustrations of life in the Navy. Sailor Armstrong was under detention in the lunacy ward of the U. S. Naval Hospital.

After some discussion, the Navy doctors admitted that Armstrong was not seriously insane, but only too oddly behaved to serve in the U. S. Navy. His chief oddity was that he was inclined to go off into fits of laughter that lasted for hours. He could be quieted only by powerful drugs.

The officer in charge of the Naval base agreed to release him into my custody with three provisos. I was to give him employment on my weekly paper; to provide sleeping quarters for him in my house; and to do all I could to keep his novel from being published.

At the dinner table welcoming the new literary find were Margaret Anderson, Sherwood Anderson, Burton Rascoe (the critic), and several opera singers whose names I have forgotten. And Bodenheim.

A discussion of music circled the table despite Bodenheim's insistence that the art of music had no relation to the art of conversation. His further efforts to swing the talk around to a discussion of himself, or at least, of poetry in general, were ignored. But literary find John Armstrong suddenly sided with the poet.

"Mr. Bodenheim is right," said Armstrong, "one doesn't talk about music. One listens to it."

Armstrong left the table and headed for the phonograph in the living room. The music he selected for listening was Chaliapin's record "The Song of the Flea" from Boito's opera *Mefistofele.*

In the middle of the record Chaliapin unlooses a burst of Satanic laughter, for a half minute that seems like an hour. Sailor Armstrong kept putting the needle back and playing the passage over and over. Finally, rolling his pants up to his knees (why, I don't know) Armstrong joined Chaliapin in his laughter. Putting the needle back to replay the passage, Armstrong finally outlaughed the great baritone in range and volume.

We all listened and watched from the dining table.

"A fascinating sort of dementia," someone said.

"It is rarely you see an American writer," said Margaret Anderson, "who is not hopelessly sane."

There were other comments about the laughing genius with the rolled-up pants whom I had been clever enough to add to my paper's staff. Please, we were very young that night.

It was all too much for Bodenheim. At last our lonesome poet made a canny bid for our attention. Having emptied his tenth wineglass, he proceeded to eat it. He bit off chunks of his fragile goblet, chewed and swallowed the bits of glass as if they were the finest of desserts.

The diners turned one by one to watch the poet's amateur and gory performance as a glass eater.

"Good God!" someone said, "you'll kill yourself swallowing that glass. You're a poet, not a circus freak."

"Every poet is both," Bodenheim answered aloofly.

He continued to talk of poetry, and to recite some of his own latest work, holding the diners fascinated by the stream of blood and words from his mouth.

A half hour later, Bodenheim's triumph was completed. A doctor arrived to inject a powerful drug into John Armstrong, who had never stopped laughing.

Our literary find went back that night to the detention ward at the Naval base. Bodenheim, after some minor medical attention, remained as my sole colleague on the *Literary Times*.

* * *

Publisher Horace Liveright came to Chicago to scout for new writers. Liveright had a lean, medieval face. His large, dark eyes looked on authors with an enthusiasm rare in publishers. He thought writers were elves and genii. He never wearied of listening to their boasts or loaning them money. His only misbehavior toward his authors was his attitude toward their mistresses. He did his best to lure them to bed, and sometimes succeeded.

In his suite in the newly built Drake Hotel, Liveright listened to Bodenheim's true story of a prostitute he had known and whom he deemed the finest of human beings. Bogie was trying to land a job for his paragon of a street walker.

"Believe me, she is a perfect typist, and," the poet said, "if you dressed her up correctly she would contribute an exquisite air to any office."

"You must write her story as a book for me," said Liveright. "I have never heard anything more moving. I'll give you a thousand-dollar advance right now."

Liveright wrote out a thousand-dollar check to Maxwell

Bodenheim, and the poet watched the pen move as if he were looking at an incredible feat of magic. When the check was signed, Bogie stood up and asked in a hushed voice, "Can you tell me, please, where the bathroom is?"

Bogie was shown the right door. We waited a half hour for the new Liveright author to emerge. Horace became nervous.

"I never saw such happiness in any author's eyes," he said. "I couldn't help looking at him when I was signing the check. He sat there like a man bewitched. Hadn't you better go see if anything's wrong? He may have had some sort of collapse."

I entered the bathroom. Bogie was standing over the toilet, all set to urinate, but unfunctioning. Perplexity was in his face, and some pain.

Over the toilet seat was a cane-woven cover, the latest thing in stylish toilet décor. Pointing at the half-inch holes in the ornamental cane cover, poet Bodenheim said,

"I can't possibly pee through that small aperture. Maybe rich people can, after considerable practice. But I don't want to start practicing in Mr. Liveright's bathroom. If I wet that elegant cane seat, he's likely to think of me as a vandal, and tear up that little old check he has written out in my name."

I showed Bogie how to outwit the cane seat by lifting it out of the way, and came back to Horace with the story of the confused urinator.

"What an honest, unspoiled human being," publisher Liveright said. "We have no natural geniuses of that kind in New York."

Bodenheim, putting the check reverently into his brief case, said,

"I give you my word of honor that I shall surpass Victor Hugo as a novelist."

*   *   *

Bodenheim wrote a few novels for Liveright, *Georgia May, Replenishing Jessica, Naked on Roller Skates.* They were hack work with flashes of tenderness, wit, and truth in them, and some verbal fireworks in every chapter.

He spoke of his novels without enthusiasm.

"Millions of people are reading my prose effusions," he said—millions and thousands were the same general number to Bogie—"but I'm not actually happy. I am returning shortly to writing poetry."

He did. His royalty checks dwindled. His brief fame as an odd, erotic novelist evaporated. And the Greenwich Village Bodenheim emerged. A homeless wino started reading his poems in saloons and picking up the pennies and nickels thrown to him. Occasionally an editor bought one of his poems and rewarded him with a twenty-five-dollar check.

He continued trying to strike it rich by entering all the poetry contests. Prizes ranging from a hundred to a thousand dollars were to be snatched by the winners.

Bodenheim had entered, since his youth, 223 such contests, and been defeated by other poets in all of them. He used to sign his letters to editors, "*Maxwell Bodenheim, 224th ranking U.S.A. poet.*"

The Greenwich Village Bodenheim had no allure for me. I preferred to remember the Chicago version. One rainy day I ran into Bogie on Broadway. His face was gaunt, most of his teeth were gone. But there were somethings unchanged about him. He was wearing the same army overcoat, carrying the same worn and bulging brief case; and his eyelids still fluttered disdainfully when he spoke.

In a saloon, Bogie showed me the poems he had written in the last ten years. They covered several hundred pages of typing. They were no longer poems full of fragile and unexpected metaphors, poems that used to seem written not by a human being but by some brilliant Jack-of-Diamonds.

The new Bodenheim output in his ten New York years was full of coherently phrased love for shop girls, laborers, and all underdogs and castaways. There was no hint in them of the poet's own travail, of his despairs, hungering days, attempted suicides. Written during hangovers, during illnesses that kept him out of saloons that still tolerated his presence, they were the poems of an observer, never a victim. They were also in sonnet form, and rhymed. But their unexpected imagery was unchanged.

Unchanged also his talk. Not a cackle, grimace, or snap of phrase missing. We rode to my home in Nyack. The rain turned into a thick snowfall.

I wanted him to stay overnight, but he couldn't. His wife, Grace, was ill and needed his love and attention. In the snow-clouded doorway, Bogie said, his voice full of mockery:

"I don't suppose you can imagine anyone loving me or needing my love. I am a scarecrow without teeth. Well, let me tell you something, my little Gracie loves me and needs me. As much as any man is loved or needed in the world. And she knows I will always come home to her, to take care of her."

A half-drunken Bodenheim left Nyack, without staying for dinner. His overcoat pockets bulged with loot stolen from my dressing room — socks, shorts, ties, shirts, a pair of patent-leather shoes, and pajama tops. He had been too proud to ask for them.

During our talk before he went, we had made a literary arrangement. Bogie was to send me every week a new poem or two pages of prose on any subject. In return I would send him a check for thirty-five dollars.

The arrangement lasted for a year, possibly two. I never saw Bogie again but his two pages of prose and an occasional poem arrived every week. Separate from them came a letter acknowledging the receipt of his weekly check, or protesting politely its nonappearance.

These letters, some of which I didn't lose, contain one of the most desperate self-portraits I have ever read; the portrait of an unwanted talent; penniless, almost rotted away with liquor and calamities — but still as proud and articulate as any prime minister.

Since the time Mencken identified Maxwell Bodenheim as "a faker and a stupid clown" almost nothing has been written of the poet or his work. In the U.S. an unsuccessful poet is more disdained than even a bankrupted industrialist.

In these letters a first voice sounds for Bodenheim — his own.

> *Care of Harvey Barnes*
> *R.F.D. No 1*
> *Woodstock, New York.*

Dear Marie,*

You did not answer my last letter so perhaps The Mountebank has reached you with some of his subtle poison. I am rather ill, with a touch of T.B. — the result of long years in stuffy, quaintly odored, cheap rooming houses — and I am penniless with no strength to go out and fight for nickels. If you could send me fifty dollars I might get through the next month, as I cannot impose on the people I am with any longer. At any rate, you will not respond with a note announcing the invisible enclosure of 200 dollars — an ironic relief. I do not expect to hear from you, of course — my attitude toward all humans is invincibly cynical just now. However . . .

With all earnestness,

MAXWELL BODENHEIM

* [Marie Armstrong Hecht — for a while.]

January 11th
10 Montague Terrace
Brooklyn 2, N.Y.

Dear Ben and Rose:

Thanks very much for the January Eighth cheque which came this week. Yesterday, I attended a party given by the Doubleday and Knopf firms in honor of the publication of an anthology entitled, "Poems of the Negro," edited by Langston Hughes, and "One Way Ticket," Langston's latest book of verse. I was invited because two of my poems to Negroes are included in the anthology. The affair was held in the Downtown Art Gallery which occupies two spacious floors, and the large assemblage was rather evenly divided between White and Negro highbrows, male and female. I was entranced by the talk confined entirely to literary small-talk, social gossip and airy witticisms. It was weird to turn from this atmosphere and remember the existence of a grim, portentous, menacing, outside world. I was treated with nice friendliness and responded in turn, but . . . I felt a bit puzzled as I left the Gallery and walked to the subway . . . Best regards to both of you from Grace and myself.

As ever,

MAXWELL

February 24th
10 Montague Terrace
Brooklyn 2, N.Y.

Dear Ben and Rose:

Thanks very much for the weekly cheque which came yesterday . . . The Fellows in American Letters of the Library of Congress have just awarded a one thousand dollar poetry prize to Ezra Pound. This honoring of a shallow, pompous, race-hating, heartless old wraith of a fascist — who was a trivially eccentric snob long before fascism came into being — represents a brazen insult to American poets

and poetry. Reading through a list of the judges in the
account printed by the New York times, Louise Bogan,
Conrad Aiken, T.S. Eliot, Allen Tate, et al, I failed to see
the inclusion of a single person known to me as a Jewish
creative writer. Another writer apologetically confessed to
me that the entire situation was a bit odd, and I replied
that it was as odd as a pane of transparent glass . . . If
you can send the next cheque so that it will reach us on
the coming Monday, we will greatly appreciate it. We hope
that your book is proceeding smoothly and we both send
both of you our best regards,

As ever,
MAXWELL

10 Montague Terrace, Brooklyn N.Y.
Saturday

Dear Ben:

Glad you like the two poems. After reading them — and
I have twenty more, just as good and written during the
past half year — you can readily see why poetry of this kind
doesn't have a snowball's chance on the equator with American magazines and papers. Five weeks ago I sold one poem
to *Esquire* and two months ago "Poetry" — once Harriet
Monroe's pet — accepted another. Never before in the history of American print have magazines shrunk to such a
low level. Formerly, on the cultural field, we had *The Dial,
The Freeman, The Double Dealer, The Little Review, The
Seven Arts Monthly,* etc. Now we have exactly nothing, and
after the war, with the attendant dull, semi-Fascist sneak-
punch which certain men will try to put over here, it will
be even worse . . . I have been very ill with neuritis,
arthritis, and a slightly frayed heart. Put a nice snarl, dag-
ger, sympathy for underlings, and a searching grin into that
new book you're writing. In the midst of my material flirta-
tions with a park bench as a future couch, and my semi-
starvations, I'm glad that a few men are still alive to write

edged truth and matters generally offensive to pigs, foxes, and rodents. Despite our personal differences, I have always liked your work and can honestly say that I've never slammed it. Do write very soon. I'm enclosing another poem. As ever,

BOGIE

When I say I've never slammed your work, Count Bruga, of course, is excepted.

P.S. Give my very best wishes to Rose. I hope it's a girl!

SONNET

To eavesdrop on the chatting of the air
With foliage in a glade disrobed by dawn;
To watch within a forest's ruffled lair
The light discreet alertness of a fawn;
To spy the tossing venture of a brook,
Or finger flowers with a quiet respect,
Or cast a wistfully rewarded look
Upon a tall tree sturdy and erect —
These are experiences that find and frame
A question filled with unexplained distress.
Oh why do men spend centuries to tame
And slowly conquer outside wilderness
While all their wilderness of heart and mind
Remains disrupted, obstinate and blind?

MAXWELL BODENHEIM

TO ISRAELI JEWS AND TO GENTILES

The scapegoats of the centuries have shaped
A slow enduring miracle from pain.
Their spirits, tortured, villified and raped,
Now climb, embattled, fused in growing gain.
They claim no glory, exaltation, might.
Plain hearts and brains with ordinary faults,
They move with common Gentiles seeking light
Against dark ignorances and assaults.

And yet, this spread of understanding still
Confronts sly hypocrites and hate-filled groups.
Too often, words of tolerance and good will
Hide slinking Gentile poisoners and their dupes.
Intelligence can never yawn or flinch.
It must fight hard for progress, inch by inch.

MAXWELL BODENHEIM

10 Montague terrace
Brooklyn 2, N.Y.
Wednesday.

Dear Ben and Rose:

Your weekly cheque came yesterday afternoon. Thanks a lot. The Cleveland Plain Dealer mailed me a clipping of a tiny seventeen-line review of the Selected Poems which states that the poems are uneven but "there are times when Maxwell Bodenheim rises to heights from which he cannot be dislodged by any legitimate criticisms. His influence on his important era — from 1914 to today — will be acknowledged in the end." Seems that some of the out of town boys and girls haven't heard of the Gotham brush-off and indifference bloc, or are too fair to subscribe to it. Glad to note that Swan Song is contradicting its title and holding on in a lingering prelude. Now that O.P.A. has been murdered, the cute black hogs can give themselves a coat of whitewash and emerge as legally sanctioned white swine. The big bloaters were also getting envious of their underworld half-brothers and decided to end the intolerable situation. Capitalism will eventually crumple under the weight of its greedy clichés, ponderously frayed hypocrisies and unholy marriage between race-hating poisons and commercial rivalries for world markets, and the result will be a better life for the many or a survival of a few dazed wandering semi-savages. The finale may not take place for two or three hundred years because the old top hog is tricky, resourceful and astute . . . Well, fond regards to you and Rose and best wishes to your daughter. As ever,

BOGIE

Wednesday
10 Montague Terrace
Brooklyn 2, N.Y.

Dear Rose and Ben:

When I opened the letter in the hotel lobby and took out the two cheques, I wept a little, and the hotel clerks and bellboys regarded me with a sort of suspicious and puzzled aloofness, wondering whether they were witnessing a mysterious ham act or deep emotion. Thanks very, very much to both of you. The landlady accepted the money with an amazed, sullen manner — the mien of a baffled wolf — though she had to be verbally polite and there is nothing else that she can inflict now . . . I hope that you have read my short stories and will tell me whether they are good or bad. This is one of the very few times that I have ever been rescued from a greased tightrope several feet away from the edge of the chasm and I'm still a bit shaky. Thanks again. I do hope that I'll have a chance to talk to both of you soon. My second play, "The Elusive Answer," was presented to Mike Todd two weeks ago and I'm crossing fingers and hoping for a miracle. Fond regards to both of you and best wishes to your daughter.

As ever,

BOGIE

Monday, September 8th
10 Montague Terrace,
Brooklyn 2, N.Y.

Dear Ben and Rose:

Thanks very much for the weekly cheque which came today. In an ancient Chinese tale, the poet, Li Tai Po, recited his personal woes to another creator much more endowed with worldly goods. The other quizzically remarked that the list represented a monotone of misfortunes calling for an equally undeviating amount of compassion close to the exhaustion of boredom. Li Tai Po replied that the ability of two monotones to blend harmoniously represented a test of the presence or absence of suppleness, depth and variety in friendship . . . The building in which we live has been sold, and the landlady, only a lessee, must vacate the premises. We have been told by the city renting commission that we can remain, after her departure, and strive to make arrangements with the new owner. The hitch is that the furniture in our place belongs to her, and she has offered to sell it to us and asked us to name a figure. So, we must either purchase the furniture, or buy new chairs, beds, tables, etc., or be left with a bare apartment and the floor for sleeping quarters. With a new abode practically impossible to find in the present housing shortage, this leaves us in a dire dilemma. One hundred and fifty dollars including the coming rent would solve our abrupt and entirely unexpected problem. I trust that you will not be irritated at my having at least presented the above facts to you. The deadline for the furniture purchase is September Fifteenth.

Hoping to hear from you, we send our fond regards and best wishes to your little daughter.

As ever,

BOGIE

10 Montague Terrace,
Brooklyn 2, N.Y.
March Tenth

Dear Ben and Rose:

Thanks very much for the weekly cheque which came today via air-mail.

I spend fifteen minutes every Sunday listening to ex-Mayor La Guardia over the radio, as he lambasts the thirty per cent loan sharks: the real-estate gang blocking sorely needed housing construction until rent ceilings are abolished and rentals can skyrocket; the food-firms and their clammy, infinitesimal tricks; the professional gambler-crooks and their crocodile lurkings, etc. The guy is shrill, stuttering, oldmaidish and sometimes banal, but his sheer guts, defiance, and pounding away at little disagreeable truths and facts are marvelous in comparison to the dreary, smooth, covered-up hacks among other radio commentators. If he is connected to the Coast, you ought to tune in on him some Sunday noon. His New York station is WJZ.

Fond regards to both of you and best wishes to your child.

As ever,

BOGIE

Dear Ben and Rose Hecht:

Please forgive my delay in thanking you for the one hundred dollar cheque — a delay caused by the fact that I've been having a tough time of it. I was compelled to leave the Brooklyn address where dearest Grace and I lived for so many years. At present, I am staying with surface friends in a New York City, but I have no privacy there, since my bed is in their living room and their children are prying and noisy. A lone drab room in a third rate hotel would repel me. I have searched for a locked-door private room with a nice family — I would eat my meals outside — but that is difficult to find. On the night before the morning on

which Grace died in the flesh only, I gave a lecture before
an evening English class at Washington Irving High School
in New York and hurried back to Grace. Our apartment-
door lock was broken and Grace closed the door with an
inner latch which I could lift from the outside with a knife.
On this night she had forgotten and locked the door. Very
sick, she had to crawl on hands and knees to open the
door. I telephoned her doctor but, since we owed him ten
dollars, he refused to come and sent a substitute, who in-
jected morphine into her aching legs and assured me that
she would fall asleep and survive. At the beginning of the
next morning when she was gasping for breath, I phoned
him again, desperately, and he came . . . when it was too
late. Then he had the nerve to stand in the doorway and
ask me if I was going to pay him. If the landlord had
heeded our pleas to repair the lock, Grace might still be
alive in the flesh. The vicious heartlessness of most human
beings appalls me . . . I am not asking for money and I
sincerely mean this, but if I could have a quiet talk with
both of you, soon, I would deeply appreciate it, as I seem
to be going to pieces.

As ever,
MAXWELL BODENHEIM
BOGIE

About Grosz

What a night that was. December 30, 1918, Berlin.

It snowed. The heavy snowfall muted some gunfire a few blocks beyond my Hotel Adlon window.

I had arrived that afternoon as foreign correspondent for the Chicago *Daily News*. I was twenty-four, spoke no German and knew as little about European politics as it was possible for an American newspaperman to know. In those days that was a considerable vacuum.

It was midnight. Looking out of the window at the foreign snowfall, I wondered who was shooting whom. Boom boom . . . rat-a-tat-tat. The war was over, so it must be a revolution.

I put on a cap I had brought along to make me inconspicuous while covering foreign events. It turned out to be the only cap in Berlin.

The phone rang. A Herr Doktor Karl von Doehman was in the lobby, wishing to see me. Tell him to come up. Von Doehman was the only German I knew in the ex-Kaiser's land. I had met him the night before on the train from Amsterdam. The train was jammed. We rode all night standing up like vertical sardines. Herr Doktor Doehman, packed against me, was returning from Amsterdam with a newly purchased opera hat.

He was a tall fellow and spoke English. I asked him, as any Chicago reporter would, if he was carrying bombs in the hatbox he was adroitly protecting. He showed me the new opera hat. During his three years' service in the German army, he had dreamed of owning such a hat and wearing it at social events.

"As a surgeon and a poet I attend many social affairs," he said. What sort of poetry did he write? Standing chin to nose in the packed train he recited:

'The moonlight touches her sleeping neck and elongates it into an interesting plumbing fixture.'

Dr. Doehman came in. He was taller than he had seemed on the train; six foot three. He was about thirty years old, dark-haired, well-built, and as good-looking as a movie star. He was wearing his opera hat.

I was glad to see him. He could tell me, perhaps, who was shooting whom in the heavy snowfall. Was it a revolution of some sort?

Some people might call it a revolution, said my opera-hatted visitor, but in reality it was only a few more corpses being piled up around the altar of nonsense.

"I shall find out for you what has happened," said Dr. Doehman, "so you will be able to send your paper a report in the morning. But first may I have the honor of introducing you to the greatest man in Germany. He is your own age, twenty-four, as you told me."

"Do I have to dress up?"

"No, your cap is sufficiently correct."

We rode in a droshky through the snow-filled night to the habitat of George Grosz.

SOME MEMORIES OF A FAVORITE DON QUIXOTE

Grosz lived four flights up in a dismal tenement. Dr. Doehman stopped outside a door on which English and German sentences were painted. The English one read: *Danger! Keep Out!*

Dr. Doehman banged and kicked patiently at the door for a half hour. Grosz, he explained, was a profound sleeper.

The door opened. A lean young man in a blue flannel nightgown looked out, sleepily. He was sharp featured, brown-haired, pinkish skinned. I was introduced to Herr George Grosz.

"Are you a political leader of some kind?" I asked.

In the droshky Dr. Doehman had given me no further information about "Germany's greatest man," on whom we were calling at 1 A.M.

"Yes, indeed, you may from a certain broad point of view describe me as a political leader," Herr George Grosz answered. "On the other hand, such a description could well be misleading. Don't you agree, Herr Doktor?"

We were in a large room that seemed totally unfurnished. I finally detected an army cot, a chair, and a painter's easel in the shadowy room. Hundreds of canvases and slabs of cardboard stood on the floor against the walls.

So many years ago, yet I remember Grosz's talk as if he were standing in front of me in his blue flannel nightgown, and speaking his words now.

"My political activities are, so to speak, antipolitical," said Grosz in an English that seemed both mocking and pompous, and that was never to change in the next thirty-five years. "I am opposed to all politics and, naturally, politicians, also. You may say, I am opposed also to art and any other so-called manifestation of beauty, including, of course, music, toe dancing, and poetry."

I'll cut the meeting short, although it is one I am fond of reliving in full, on sleepless nights.

Grosz was an artist, a combination of caricaturist in ink and water color, and a realist in oil painting. He was co-chairman with the Bavarian artist, Titus Tautz, of the German branch of the Dadaists; a sentence, there, that sounds as if Grosz had made it up.

Dadaism was a movement launched in Zurich in 1914 by a group of international artists. None of its launchers knew exactly what it was about. Nevertheless a score of Dadaist leaders took over in various countries; Tzara in Paris, Dombotski in Vienna, Gellitti in Florence. And Grosz in Berlin.

I understood the movement somewhat, after hearing it explained scores of times by Grosz, Doehman, Tautz, and other talented followers. It was anything that any member chose to think it was; a sort of personally adjustable revolution. Thus it offered battle to old myths, old formulas, and old definitions of beauty. The fighting was heaviest on this last front. Artists have a compulsion for attacking each other almost as deep as that of believers in God. Artists stop short of burning each other at the stake or lopping off each other's heads by the gross. But they sound as ferocious as theologians.

Dadaism was an attack on everything that had hardened into convention, on the stale tastes of mankind. It was a half-comic upheaval against such uncomic matters as patriotism, idealism, and human stagnation. The Dadaists took on no less than the world as their enemy. They plotted to ridicule its bad manners out of existence; to let fly at the cultured public of Everywhere; at the smugness and correctness entrenched behind all the magazines, books, newspapers, university professors, statesmen, critics, and sofa cushion menders; at the whole of modern civilization surrounded by its terrifying moat of platitude.

This sounds a bit top heavy as an explanation. Indeed, I prefer George Grosz's statement on the aims of the Dadaists.

"We are, shall I say, revolutionists," said Grosz, "whatever is more important than one human being we are prepared to revolt against."

Dr. Doehman added,

"Without anarchy the world is certain to become a vast plaza for government buildings, a planet of museums."

"Our final battle cry," said Grosz, "will be, 'down with the Dadaists.' Also 'down with Dadaism.' At that time, I assure you, I will be proud to fight as a traitor, which is the secret of progress."

The Dadaism I met in Berlin may have been related to the disillusion of a lost war. But not for Grosz. He was a full-fledged revolution, a simoon of ink and water colors ripping through German streets.

I brought a photographer to his barren room and came away with two hundred negatives of his as yet unpublished output. Two years later we displayed the photographs of the Grosz drawings in the large window of Covici-McGee's Book Store in Chicago. I had written captions on the drawings. They were strung across the window on a half-dozen clotheslines.

Washington Street filled up with a mob of art lovers. Loop traffic was tied up. A few store windows were caved in by the crush. Mounted police had to be called to scatter the host of art fanciers.

There was no pornographic lure in the Grosz drawings. They gave off an aura of hell.

I'll describe one of the two hundred pictures we hung in the Covici-McGee window. On a rooming house bed lies a female figure, drawn in quick and tidy lines; a sort of Morse code of a female. Her dress is rumpled and hoisted to her hips. Her plump young thighs are exposed.

It would be a wanton pose, except for the fact that the young woman is without a head. It has just been chopped off, and fallen out of sight behind the bed.

The ax-wielder stands over a washbowl, fastidiously cleaning his hands. His shirt is off. His suspenders hang amiably from his trousers. He was evidently undressing to join the plump thighs in the bed, when something caused him to alter his plans. As he washes his hands, he casts a grateful look at the weapon he just used.

Over the doorway is a horseshoe, with silk bow tied to it.

I captioned this drawing "The Irritating Bride."

Years later, Grosz corrected me.

"They were not married," he said.

I had never before seen such drawings as I saw in Grosz's Berlin studio, and have not seen the like of them to this day. Fever-thin lines, quaint spurts of ink that seemed to crawl on the paper, tipsy walls, spidery streets, leering windows; a half-ghostly goulash of breasts, buttocks, thighs, drooling mouths, murderous eyes, crafty fat necks, and all the strut and coarseness of the overfed subhumans who ran the German world and sported in its German cafes — these were in the Grosz drawings.

Grosz, as fine a draftsman as Delacroix, and as disillusioned an eye as Daumier, omitted nine tenths of anatomy and structure from his drawings. The result was a "tenth" full of nightmare. It was life that was being violated. His figures scratched at your eyes. Immorality, heavy lipped and heavy uddered, rolled a bovine eye at army officers and financiers who sat belching aloofly on their large, authoratative rumps. Lust, gluttony, brutality, and all the tricks of wearied evil snickered out of the half humans who kissed and killed one another in a world that looked like a demented strawberry box.

And there were scores on scores of water colors. The rage that Grosz put into his fever thin lines he instilled somehow in his pink, red, green, and purple tints. His painted clothes, curtains, flags, bedspreads, carpets looked as if some disease were consuming them. Rage, rage was in every inch of Grosz's work. Every line and hue cried out with Joyce Cary's hero "The world's a dirty dog!"

Yet during all the years I knew Grosz I never heard him speak an unkind word about anyone, or anything. Except of the Nazism of his German countrymen.

"They are fine people," Grosz said, "but they are quick to catch the disease of anti-humanity which is very close to many people, but my poor Germans are unusually susceptible. I think it is, on the whole, because of their poor elimination. Yes, I am sorry to say, I think Germany is a headquarters for constipation."

Doehman and I played piano and violin duets in my hotel parlor. Grosz sat on top of the piano, singing songs of his own. We toured among the Officer Clubs where the aristocrat perverts gathered to exchange data and addresses. We ate in slum kitchens behind Alexander Platz, and went to macabre parties where Lesbians beat up college boys and bemedaled colonels sat with painted children in their laps. We attended political conferences, Grosz pretending to be my interpreter. Wherever we went, Grosz was a man at work. You could feel him sketching, sketching in his head; absorbing expressions, gestures, of pompous, oily officials. And there were officials everywhere you turned in 1919 Berlin. Officials jabbering as if it were always the week before election; and behind the jabbering a new German army being built up that was to challenge the world again to mortal combat.

Occasionally Grosz was arrested and stuck in a military jail for a few days. This would happen after one of his caricatures in the Dadaist newspaper had pinked an important government personage. The newspaper was a four-page gazette, four feet square. It was impossible for one pair of hands to hold it open.

"We have designed our newspaper," said Grosz, "so couples will have something intellectual to do in bed."

One of Grosz's caricatures that earned him a week in Moabit Prison was of Count von Rantzau. The Count was Military Minister of the new Ebert-Scheidemann German Social Democratic Party. General Gustav Noske was then in charge of rebuilding the surrendered but undestroyed German Army. Rantzau and Noske were able twelve years later to hand over to Hitler a magnificently equipped and disciplined fighting host prepared under the mask of German Socialism.

Grosz was aroused by the first bellicose strut of postwar

Germany. He attacked its chief strutters, among them Count von Rantzau. A caricature, two feet square, appeared on the front page of the Dadaist gazette. It showed Rantzau standing behind his desk, banging it with his fist. A pair of toy cannons were on the desk. The Count's heavy face was as full of fierceness and power as the fist that banged the desk. But the powerful Count's fly was open, and a pathetically tiny male organ drooped out of it. There was no caption to the picture.

"George is out of bondage," Dr. Doehman told me. "We are preparing a great Festival of the Arts. Admission, the equivalent of five American dollars. You, however, will have a box, free."

"I'm coming alone," I said, "I don't need a box."

"It will be safer," Dr. Doehman explained.

It was a large concert hall. Huge, excitingly painted posters advertising the Great Art Festival had signaled for weeks from hundreds of Berlin walls and fences. The posters proclaimed the FIRST GERMAN POST-WAR RENAISSANCE OF THE ARTS. ADMISSION, 20 GOLD MARKS. FORMAL DRESS REQUIRED.

I sat in my box and looked down on an audience of Berlin's most distinguished citizens in their finest military and civilian plumage.

The ornate assemblage of culture lovers looked patiently on the brightly lighted, bare stage. A figure in a frock coat and a yellow straw hat walked onto the stage.

I didn't recognize Grosz for several minutes, because he spoke in German and was in black-face.

Another man in a dress suit appeared, carrying a cello. He sat down on a kitchen chair and started tuning his instrument. During the tuning Grosz executed what he fancied was a Negro jig. The tuning over, both performers exited. There was no applause.

My tall friend, Dr. Doehman, appeared next, in tails and opera hat. He held up a hand for silence and then cried out the motif for the evening. I knew enough German by that time to make it out.

"Art is in danger!" Dr. Doehman announced.

The black-face Grosz rushed from the wings and roared at the audience another warning:

"Take your foot out of the butter before it is too late."

A series of acts followed. Grosz, Doehman, and Tautz, up from Munich for the Art Festival, did the announcing. I remember a few of them. There was a race between a girl at a sewing machine and a girl at a typewriter. Grosz fired a starter's gun. The girls began sewing and typing at top speed. The sewing machine operator was pronounced the winner. She received a set of false whiskers, and went off the stage, proudly wearing them. There was no applause.

The first "Pan-Germanic Poetry Contest" followed. Eleven seedy-looking fellows shuffled out on the stage. They wore large ribbon badges with their entry numbers on them. Several of them were barefoot. They were introduced by Doehman as Germany's leading poets. A twelfth figure appeared and was identified as a *gepäcktraeger* (a baggage smasher). He and the eleven poets were to compete for a grand prize.

Grosz appeared and fired his starter's gun. The eleven poets and the red cap began to recite their twelve different poems, simultaneously, at the top of their voices. They made gestures, brushed tears from their eyes, held hands over their hearts.

At the height of the impassioned static from the poets, Grosz fired his gun as a finishing signal. Dr. Doehman strode onto the stage and announced the contest was a draw. The cellist appeared, sat down, and started tuning his instrument, again. Grosz repeated his jig.

There was also a "Recital for the Eye of Modern Music." This event had been specially advertized in the festival posters: BEETHOVEN, BACH ARE DEAD — BUT MUSIC MARCHES ON.

Three girls in tights appeared. They placed a dozen large canvases, one by one, on an easel. Each canvas contained the drawing of a single musical note.

Grosz joined me in my box.

"It is a great success, is it not," he said, trying to speak in Negro dialect. "Someday, perhaps, we will bring our Festival of the Arts to Chicago. I was there with my parents as a child. For a visit, you understand. I remember it very vividly, the Chicago Beach Hotel and everything." This was a lie. Grosz liked to imagine he had seen the United States in his early years. He doted on anything American. While in the Army during the war, he had collected from prisoners some hundred copies of *The Saturday Evening Post*. He spent nights studying the magazine's advertisements. He considered American advertising the most honest form of expression developed by the human species.

In the box, he went on,

"I am very happy tonight. I have fallen in love with an exceedingly fine young lady, the one who put F sharp on exhibition. She is a typist. It was her first appearance in tights, that is, to an audience. In private she undresses the same as all women do, of every age. But it is not her nudity I am in love with, but her name. Her name is Eva."

Grosz darted off. The Dadaist battle cries of art in danger and a foot too long in the butter began rising from different parts of the concert hall.

Finally, the audience started its counterrevolution. Officers drew guns and fired at the stage. Police and soldiery appeared. High officials demanded the arrest of the hooligans who had swindled and mocked Berlin's elite. But there was no one to arrest. The Dadaists had melted into the spring night.

*   *   *

A few years later in Chicago I received a wedding invitation from Grosz. It was a postal card with a Grosz drawing on it. The drawing showed a shapely young woman sitting naked at a typewriter. Standing behind her, leering over her nude shoulder, was an excellent likeness of Grosz. The card read: *Eva and I are being married any day. You are invited. George Grosz.*"

*   *   *

Grosz and Eva came to New York in the early '30s. Grosz painted. Eva cooked, kept house, had two children, and moved to Bayside, Long Island. Grosz's fame as an oil painter increased. Artists and art dealers were excited over the realism of his paintings. He was hailed as a master of texture, form, construction. Renown drifted into his life, and enough money came with it to add an automobile, that he could never drive, to his Long Island possessions.

Grosz also continued feverishly in his favorite medium, water colors; and on his favorite subjects — the bottom-of-the-heap people. But the accusation was out of his picaresque drawings, out of most of them. They were art come down from an easel, not from a cross.

Grosz's American bums, Negroes, hillbillies, strip teasers, moochers, and sundry other low-income types were no longer an alphabet of despair. The great villain had vanished from his canvases, the fat-necked, heavy-rumped Top Man who would run the world between belches. Though in exile from his native land, Grosz in an odd way was loyal to Germany. He could hate only Germans.

GUTEN ABEND, HERR GROSZ

I remember a party at the Grosz home in Bayside, Long Island, one winter's night. Rose, Charlie Lederer, and I went to it through a big snowstorm.

George and his Eva are dead. But this party still goes on in my head. Lederer said to me recently about this twenty-year-ago party, "Do you remember that night in George Grosz's house? It was the most wonderful party I've ever attended." Rose agreed.

This put the Grosz party ahead of a thousand parties in Chicago, Hollywood, New York, and Paris, and Rome — for the three of us.

For that night Grosz assembled in his Bayside home the Dadaist clan of his youth. Not all of them — a sprinkling. Not Doehman, but a professor of philosophy at the Berlin University, Dr. Minona. In his Berlin days Dr. Minona used to leave his university quarters at midnight and go walking for hours in the dark, silent streets. He walked with a cornet to his lips, filling the night with piercing notes.

"Dr. Minona has a Gabriel complex," Grosz explained as we walked in Berlin one night with the cornet-tooting professor. The police never interfered. They knew who was making the noise, a Herr professor too distinguished for their attentions.

Present that night in Bayside was also a famed professor of mathematics. He had participated in the Berlin Festival of Arts as its head slogan-shouter. And there were a dozen other plumpish, middle-age fellows, exiles like Grosz from youth and from their native land. There was also a sprinkling of Americans of some note. But I have forgotten their names.

And there was Eva, dark eyed and gentle smiling as she had been in her tights at the Berlin Festival, and only a few pounds heavier. Eva seated us at a twelve-foot table piled with a kaleidoscope of meats, chickens, cheeses, fish, salads, pancakes, bakeries, sauces, and liquor bottles — a table that would have set Brueghel's brush to flying over a canvas. And Eva's remarkable handmade amber lamp shades cast a golden glow over the hullabaloo of her table.

Grosz didn't sit down. He stood against the wall looking at the merry, food-swamped table.

"My father was a saloonkeeper." Grosz mentioned a town in Prussia, but I've lost its name. "This is how his saloon looked on a Saturday night. Food for everybody. It was a beautiful saloon. My father was a man of importance. When we had asparagus for supper, my father would eat off all the soft ends of the vegetable, first. And then his family was allowed to eat the lower halves of the asparagus stalks. A man of very interesting authority."

There was a singing contest that night between the Berlin professor of mathematics and Lederer. Lederer's voice, raised in "When Irish Eyes Are Smiling," had been known in Hollywood, New York, and Paris to shatter china plates and even porcelain candlesticks.

"I have heard, Charlie, that you have a voice of great quality," said Grosz. "Some people have informed me of the matter. Very high authorities. I am betting, however, on the professor. Get set! Go!"

The old professor selected "The Lorelei" for the contest. Lederer stuck to his "When Irish Eyes." The duet set dogs to barking in distant houses. Grosz listened blissfully. The professor won, by an honest vote of the guests.

Professor Minona, of the Gabriel complex, voted with teary eyes.

"I could once make twice as loud a noise," he sighed. "A whole city used to tremble at my cornet. Ah, youth never lasts. Nothing lasts."

This was Grosz's time of American happiness. As philosopher Minona indicated, all things vanish. Even genius is not enough to hold them. The home of the glowing lamp shades, knitted rugs, damask curtains made by Eva's clever hands, darkened with Grosz's melancholy. A sort of madness came on him at intervals. It sent him off into drinking fits.

He would retire to his studio above the garage adjoining his Bayside house, after stocking it with liquor. There he would sit day and night, drinking bottle after bottle.

But he was not alone with his mania and his bottles. Eva sat with him, and drank with him as much as she could. Instead of worrying him with her despair, she pretended to be part of his revelry. Her devotion helped lift the fogs in Grosz's head.

One morning Eva phoned me in Nyack and asked if I would come out that day to sit with George in his studio. She had become sick from her nights of kamerad drinking.

Grosz was busy when I entered his studio. A Franklin stove was aglow at one end of it.

"I am happy to see you," a red-eyed Grosz croaked, "please, have a seat and I will join you in a few minutes, maybe five at the most."

I watched Grosz head for the stove with a painting in his hand. He thrust it into the coals. It burned brightly.

"What the hell are you doing?" I asked.

"Forgive me — a few more minutes," said Grosz. "I will make a confession to you. When I feel a little bad I come up here to my studio as you know to recuperate. At a certain point of recuperation, I begin to paint pictures. The most ugly pictures you can conceive; what you might call pornographic pictures. I paint and paint, uglier and uglier pictures. Then I become sober, as you see me now, and I look at these pictures of my sickness, and I am greatly disgusted with myself. So I work, as you see me at this moment, burning them up. All of them. All the ugliness is destroyed by the fire."

I grabbed Grosz as he was making his third trip to the Franklin stove.

He carried a remarkable-looking painting in his hands. It revealed two nude, voluptuous bawds trying to excite the passions of a pair of nude male customers. The wenches were concentrated on the reluctant phalli.

I begged Grosz not to destroy the picture, but sell it to me. He refused. The existence of such an ugly picture would ruin his name forever, he explained.

"It doesn't have to be ugly," I said. "You can paint out the male customers and their appendages. And it'll be a picture of two female nudes, amazingly painted. All your nudes are usually stiff and academic. These are the livest ones you've ever done."

Grosz finally gave in. He painted out the offensive masculine details, and the men, also. For months after I had hung the picture in my Nyack house, Grosz would call up and ask me to go look at it, and turn a flashlight on it, and let him know if the original ugliness of the picture had begun to assert itself, "to show through, as it were."

As I write in a small room in New York hung with Grosz's paintings, the two fleshy bawds are still without male companions.

        ❋   ❋   ❋

Now there is a George Grosz boom. His paintings and water colors that once brought a few hundred dollars apiece are now selling for thousands of dollars.

Art booms are usually the result of art collector rivalries and shrewd art auction manipulations. I think the Grosz boom is otherwise.

It is a sort of literary boom. George Grosz's paintings and drawings have begun to cry out their stories of inhumanity, of Authority crucifying a bewildered and helpless century.

Books on books are appearing with the data and proof of past brutality, and with the forecasts of even more hideous events to come. But such books are only words that drift in and out of a reader's head, that mingle confusedly with other written words; that end up saying almost nothing.

Grosz's art is a sturdier sort of writing. Particularly the art of his Berlin years and of his Second World War years in New York. Its accusations cry out with no line of them dimmed.

I remember his always polite and kindly voice, his pleasant and always friendly look. But out of his art the rage of a prophet keeps sounding. His drawings and water colors echo his Festival slogan; not art but life is in danger.

There is one picture painted in New York in 1941. Great, festive vermillion curtains have been flung apart. Standing triumphantly in their opening, bony hands clutching the luxurious folds, is the white and grinning skeleton of Death. An incredible joy gleams about him, as he stands between the parted, vermillion curtains. The painting is called, "I Am Glad I Came Back Again."

How piddling are the angry young men who write for the stage and even most of those who write books damning the human biped for having fouled his planetary nest, how lame are their words beside the spidery lines and crawling bits of ink that the genius of Grosz left behind.

For many years I have had only two good words to say about Germans — George and Eva.

❖   ❖   ❖

13/3/33

Dear Benny!

The photos are marvellous — I look at the one like a typ[e] just out of my books. Thanks a lot.

The afternoon at yours was fine. Here I send the book of Grosz Poems, I promised to you. Enjoy it on a Sunday. All poems are written 1916–17. Then nevermore I did poetry.

My water-color show is now on. Walk in and have a look —

With shake hands

yours,

GEORGE GROSZ

Greetings to your wife!
also from Mrs. Grosz to you both

The Cambridge Hotel
60 West 68 Street

Dear Ben:

Thank you. Thank you very much for your letter. Yes I have been in Des Moines as a Guest Teacher (Cowles Foundation) Your letter was forwarded to the Art Students Lg. N.Y. Got it yesterday. Hence I didn't answer. Meanwhile I was in bed with the so called asian Flu. Saw you on the TV the other day. We liked you very much, what you had to say and the way you said it. By the way the guy who did the decorations and the lightning for Winkelberg studied once with me. (Long time ago though) Are you still at the Algonquin. I became kind of a recluse myself. Go only to town twice a week, where I have to teach in a kindergarden. Hope to see you sometime maybe in New York, after my Kindergarden lecture.

To you and Rosie my love and fondest greetings with a little nostalgia always your olde friend

GEORGE

Nb. Des Moines was pretty dull. Got acquainted with good old Karl Mattern. (he had a slight stroke, but recovered from it) he showed me old clippings among them an article of you about him. Told me too about the sculpter Szukalski and the old bohemian days in Chicago. By the way, my son

Mart plays Banjo and guitarre in a nightclub in Chicago, the Gaslightclub. So long, have to go down for dinner (Schitzel à la Holstein)

40-41 221 Street
Bayside
Long Island
October 4, 1935

Dear Bennie,

I'm back in town, just want to say hallo to you and Mrs. Hecht — o yees — glad to be back anyway — as the whole Europa looks to me pretty tense. (of course from the outside and with good American money in the pocket, as a tourist — allright — but if you listen to the undercurrents — gee!)

Now I want to ask you wether you ever got that watercolor of mine, you know, which you called "Gigolo", with the old lady and the boy next to her walking, in the background scyscrapers. I had sent it to you before I left — 3 month ago. How have you been? Just give me a word or two, will'ye? And if time allows, it would be swell to see you both again — mebbe you can drop in at our place sometime for supper and a little glas of brandy — and for a chat around the fireplace — love and greetings to you both

Yours,
GEORGE GROSZ

N.B. If you are in need sometimes of a good "handyman" sofar "settings and so" are concerned, think of me — furthermore: I opened my own school again in the "Squibb Bldg" 22 floor — please do make a bit talking about it — among your friends — just a bit "propaganda" that's it what I need to go along —

202 *Shore Road*
Douglas Manor
Long Island
July 30, 1941

Dear Benny,

I thank you VERY MUCH for the (illustration, showing box labeled "Belindas, 50 Demi Tasse"). Something of the quality of them went right into my drawings — thanks a lot —

Now, Benny, I guess I am through as far as your book goes — there is only one story left the title is: "Johnny get your gun"

With this one I made 7 new ones (seven). We have now altogether 85 drawings (which is quite something). As I intend to go away next week Wednesday for a fortnight vacation to Wellfleet — Cape Cod — please let me know if you intend to have a few more stories illustrated. I'll like to finish before I leave.

With my best greetings — to you & Rosie

as ever yours,
devoted illustrator & friend
GEORGE GROSZ

The new proofs & prints are delightful — very good

202 *Shore Road*
Douglas Manor
Long Island
January 3, 1943

Dear Benny,

I thank you very much for your fine and encouraging words. Indeed, the painting is good and it is nice to know that you have it — and treasure it. I read a good piece of you on the Jewish question in the American Mercury. Hitlerman blundered this year in Russia — sofar (as Russia is concerned) the new news are promising — Stalingrad! Maybe it is a turning point. Let's hope that the Russians keep on going. See — I throw a big party if — on[e] day — Hitlerman is out. But let's keep cool — the Germans are not defeated yet — and I know them quite well. I think he will try in the coming spring a new drive. So let's keep the good spirit and wait. Monday, Ben, there is an opening of my show at the A.A.A. Galleries — 711 Fifth Avenue — please do come at about 5 — or 6 — entirely new oils. You have not seen. Bring Rosie and if you like your friends along. Later we go to my friend E. Cohn and celebrate with a little drink. There are new oils: 1. "A mighty one, on a little outing surprised by two poets" a political painting, never shown before (sold already to Arnold B. White) very good one. 2. "The Ambassador of good will" from my Cyklus "The Thin and the Fat" (new one painted 1943) political too.

There are many other good oils — so you will have a good time anyhow — as here is a show not showing "Wald & Wiesen" pictures — Can you bring Billy Rose — maybe? (if he is in town?) I write to him extra.

What's your opinion about the polemic of Klaus Mann on "Surrealisme" — I think he brought up a few good points, didn't he. Well — that's that!

Hoping you are oke and your work coming along nicely — I remain as ever with love to you & Rosie

Your old pal,

GEORGE

You will get an invitation too — and keep your evening free please. The date is Monday the 8 of February — (you know that I always like to be in your company).

There will be furthermore: oils: "I am glad I came back again" and "I awoke in the night and I saw the house burning."

About Antheil

There's something to be said for dying young. George Antheil, the indestructible Bad Boy of Music, keeled over in his early fifties. He was possibly a bit older. I could find out from his widow, Boski (called Beshky). But that's no way to write about an intimate friend after he dies — check up on him as if he were some defunct alien.

I'll write only what I know of Georgie, as I have about his predecessors in these pages. What impresses me about my information on all of them, is how little it is.

Apparently, the mind has an unlimited supply of graves in which to bury the data of relationships — as soon as they become useless. Contrary to the report of the poets whose task it is to brighten their madrigals with something better than truth, our dead friends and dead loved ones do little haunting of our hearts. We forget them, surprisingly; and forget our own previous selves with a similar hastiness . . . The selves we shared with those who died are buried with their bones. It is as difficult to remember our past identities as to recite the names of our nation's Vice-Presidents.

The good thing to be said for dying young, or youngish, is that you leave behind a better memory of yourself, for the few who have time to remember you. There will never be a hollow-eyed, wrinkle-necked Antheil for us to see when we turn our heads for a look at the past — that glum look of a frost-bitten old orphan staring into the window of a toy shop. There will be always a fortissimo fellow bearing his name; an enviable mop of russet hair that cost him a fortune in barber fees; the body of a lightweight prize fighter, tidily dressed; and a childlike face with two expressions — a look of surprise, or a beam of pure happiness.

Such was the Antheil exterior, almost unchanged from the day he fled New Jersey for Paris, to the day some forty years later when he returned to his West End Avenue apartment in New York with a contract for a TV Christmas opera, and a touch of dizziness.

"I think I'll sit down for a while, and rest," said Georgie.

"I'll get you some hot soup," said Boski, who was as fine a cook as ever came out of Vienna.

Georgie died while Boski was in the kitchen, heating the soup.

Unlike most music composers, Antheil could write and talk with considerable intelligibility. Yet his interior remained mysterious to me. Ideas, opinions, desires were in his head, but they were little islands in a great sea of sound. Music filled his cranium. Orchestras played constantly behind his eyebrows. You could almost see the pianos, fiddles, bassoons, flutes, and kettle drums floating around in him, and sidetracking his attention from any business in hand; except eating or noticing a pretty girl who looked a little unhappy.

Music poured out of Antheil sixteen hours a day. He did nothing but write music and play it on the piano, which he made sound like a calliope in a circus parade. Driving an automobile, flying the Atlantic, watching a ball game, or drinking himself pie-eyed, George Antheil kept on writing music, carrying it in his head until he could get to paper and ink pot.

There is no Antheil boom as yet. But there's one tuning up. Antheil's capricious symphonies and furious rondos are being played more and more by adventurous orchestras.

It will take a few years for Antheil to win the laurels due him. This is because the Antheil fame was a bit spotty when he died. The Art World was miffed at Georgie. He had deserted to the movies. The rule is — you cater to the masses or you kowtow to the elite; you can't have it both ways.

But the rule is a fickle one, as are most of the edicts of snobbery. Snobbery is always ready to turn on a dime. It remains in good repute by making saints out of the heretics it burned; the while it keeps its standing as judge and jury by burning new heretics.

The fact that Antheil made a fair living writing movie music will be forgiven him soon. And the hundreds of symphonies, operas, ballets, songs, and cantatas he composed during his Hollywood residence will shed the stigma of that address, and be awarded their due by the guardians of the Arts.

Had Georgie started his career in the '50s instead of the '20s, he would have had easier going. For modernism has become quite the accepted mood and goal of all the arts in our forward plunging century. In the last fifteen years I have not met an art lover of any sort who had a derogatory word for "modernism" in music, poetry, painting, or theatrical entertainment.

But in the days when Antheil appeared on the scene, the experts were fiercely defending the world from being overrun by "charlatans." The latter included Cézanne, Matisse, Picasso, Joyce, e. e. cummings, Sandburg, Mallarmé, Stravinsky, Prokofieff, and Antheil.

It took these authorities some twenty years to relabel the "trash" and "hogwash" of these early innovators as the noblest expressions of the human spirit. Often such revaluation was done by the very same men who had done the original annihilating. The critics who hissed Bizet's *Carmen* off its first Paris stage at the Opéra-Comique in 1875 were demanding twenty years later that a statue of him be put in the opera house. They were still hissing, but now it was against composers who didn't sound like Bizet. As with the critics who booed Verdi's *La Traviata* out of La Fenice in Venice in 1853, where it made its debut. Twenty years later, they were booing Richard Wagner for not sounding like Verdi.

What turned our contemporary keepers of the orphic gates to hailing Modernism with incense pots instead of dornicks is too vast a topic for these pages. It has to do with the speed and power of our civilization that could no longer perform to waltzes.

Antheil had no bitter memories of his early days as a "modern" composer and piano virtuoso when his musical offerings set off tirades in press and salon. To the contrary, he remembered that time of battle happily.

Youth, love and the thrills of creativity were in it. Some artists are floored (or used to be) by the contempt that their out of step work excites. Antheil was not of these. The hoots of the critics only convinced him that he was on the right track.

He was not alone in this conviction. The always present handful of budding artists who call the tunes for tomorrow considered him one of them. Antheil was hailed socially and in print by James Joyce, Gertie Stein, Ezra Pound, André Gide, Jean Cocteau, Henri Matisse, Ernest Hemingway, and the like. He was proclaimed by them as the head man of musical Modernism, heir to Stravinsky; and leading Ravel and Satie by a city block.

Nearly every orchestral performance of Antheil's works produced fist fighting in the audience. Antheil enthusiasts fell upon Antheil disdainers, and a bit of blood ran in the concert halls of Paris, Munich, Prague, Berlin, and Copenhagen. He told me he was the first composer since Bizet to receive death threats through the mail. He was warned that if his *Ballet Mécanique* was played once more, he, its miserable creator, would be assassinated.

"Music lovers," said Georgie happily, "are like deeply religious people. They get terribly upset by any other religion but their own."

I am willing to take Georgie's word for it, that the music clef breeds almost as much intolerance as the altar. This is logical, for music is nearer divinity than writing or painting. If not divinity, then nearer whatever is the source of life. It shares with religion an ability to make people weep and exult for no reason. Like religion, it bypasses any intelligence we may have, and strikes at our souls.

Music is a much older language than words or picture making. Dogs, chickens, wild animals, and even fish and snakes will respond to music; whereas Shakespeare's and Rembrandt's genius will leave them cold. There is a hint in this of music's antiquity.

There is also the fact that the embattled theologians of all the different faiths except the Jews are agreed that music is constantly played and sung in heaven. There is no mention by the best-informed theologians of any oil paintings or sculpture in the Celestial Regions. And obviously nobody is writing books or making speeches in God's Kingdom. There being nothing to argue about and nothing to find out in heaven, what use is there for words?

*   *   *

Young Antheil kept himself and his Boski going as a concert pianist. It was a hazardous employment, for Antheil played chiefly his own compositions. Since he wrote for the piano as "a percussion instrument" and tried to wrench explosions rather than tunes out of it, he was constantly at loggerheads with his audiences.

My own tastes steer me away from opera houses and concert halls, as they steered me away in my boyhood from flowering into a fiddler. Modernist music has furthered my estrangement from the art. Yet I listened always with fascination to Antheil's more splintery compositions. They were as unsoothing as a punch in the nose. But you felt a musical truth in their violence. They were serenades to a tomorrow full of push-button deviltries.

Most of the modern music I have heard is a little furtive in its melody-wrecking. It doesn't quite complete its wrecker's job. It keeps hinting at old tunes and nostalgic harmonies.

Not Antheil's. No Schubert sighs or Chopin tinkles are in his modern opuses. Georgie wrote in a rocket ship.

*   *   *

At the time the young Antheil decided to tour Europe as a concert pianist and play his modernist pieces, James Joyce warned him, "They will mob you in Budapest. The Hungarians are devoted to fat music. They may try to break your fingers."

"I agree," said Gertie Stein, the Free Lunch Center for France's modernists. "Stick to Paris. Parisians never beat up an artist. They only break their hearts."

Antheil spurned the warnings. He went to Budapest and played his piano concert without suffering a scratch. Georgie remembered,

"I came out on the concert-hall stage in Budapest in tails and a white tie. Before going to the piano I faced the audience and announced in three languages, French, German, and English, 'Ladies and gentlemen, please bear in mind during my performance at the piano that I am an American from the wilds of Hoboken.' Then I removed a revolver from my pocket, a large six-shooter. I laid the gun on the piano shelf where everybody in the audience could see it. And I played without a single hiss or hoot from a single listener. I even played my *Voodoo Symphony*, and they applauded when I finished."

Antheil toured Europe's capitals thereafter. The concert halls filled up with music lovers eager to hear the American virtuoso who played his own compositions, armed to the teeth.

*   *   *

MacArthur and I lured Antheil into making money by writing music for movies. We were writing, directing, and producing our own movies in the Paramount Pictures studios in Astoria, Long Island. MacArthur and I had the dubious honor of being the first movie writers to branch out as directors and producers of their own scenarios.

We made some good movies, *The Scoundrel* and *Crime Without Passion*. But the one for which Antheil wrote the music, *Once in a Blue Moon* was a total flop. It could hardly be otherwise. Giddy with previous success, Mac-Arthur and I went "on location" to shoot this one. We summered in the woodlands adjoining the elegant town of Tuxedo, New York. With us were gypsy dancers and fiddlers, Russian clowns and aristocrat refugees, famous wrestlers and pugilists, lady vocalists, swimmers, fortune-tellers, and a gallery of admiring debutantes. They were all needed for the picture we had written.

Charlie and I directed and produced our *Blue Moon* movie in Arcadian areas lively with bicycle and swimming races, wrestling and boxing matches, drinking bouts and amorous intrigues. Through languid afternoons and moon-struck nights, music played and gypsy girls sang and danced.

I remember of our Midsummer Night's Dream troupe Nikita Balieff, Cissie Loftus, Gypsy Markoff, Hans Steinke, Jimmy Savo, Sandor Szabo, Whitney Bourne, my daughter Edwina, coerced into playing the picture's heroine; and a woodland full of nymphs and society belles from Tuxedo Park.

How note, among all these pleasantries, that nearly every member of our cast spoke with a different and nigh un-intelligible foreign accent?

Flop though the picture was, Antheil's music for it was delightful. I have never heard a merrier collection of waltzes, polkas, and background tunes than came out of its sound track. Georgie wrote melodies as if he had never heard or written a note of modern music.

There was a sway-backed old horse named Bombonetti

in the picture. What tunes Antheil wrote for this decrepit nag, Bombonetti! With belly sagging and head hanging, our weary Bombonetti seemed to be dreaming always of spring days and of nymph horses neighing in the glades.

A STROLL WITH ORPHEUS

What is a music composer? Is he of a special human tribe, a sort of throwback to man's angelic or simian origins? Is the inside of his head, with its one and a half billion brain cells, different than other peoples'?

I answer only out of George Antheil. I have met many composers, but Antheil is the only one I knew well. Instinct tells me that he was no lone specimen, but a type. If this be true, a music composer is first and foremost a husband. Without a wife to adore and cherish him, cook, scrub, launder, perform miracles with dollar bills, and wine and dine all his oboe players and undernourished disciples, a composer would blow away like dandelion fluff.

Wives are needful to writers and painters, but such moon-shooters can survive, after a fashion, without buffer mates. Not so, the music composer. Without a loyal wife to surround him like a stockade, he goes deaf, or lame or mad.

Georgie had his Boski. Her uncle was the Viennese playwright, Arthur Schnitzler. She was shapely, cultured, elegant and able to double as cook and char woman without dropping her smile. Boski cooked and cooked, produced and nurtured a son; worshiped, coddled, applauded, and forgave her Georgie through thirty-five years of living, much of which was like going over Niagara Falls in a barrel for two.

Boski listened also to each of the millions of notes Georgie wrote — and played and replayed. At home or in hotel suites, Georgie played the piano until his swollen fingers had to be stuck in a bowl of ice for healing. On such occasions, the Antheil phonograph took over, and Boski could hear her mate's music roaring from its amplifiers. Without music sounding around him, Georgie felt confused in an empty house.

As he played the piano, pummeling the hell out of its keys and stomping on the loud pedal, Georgie sang the various instrumental parts of his compositions. His half-falsetto squeal supplied horn, fiddle, flute, and drum accompaniments.

He seemed to be playing in code, but there was a hypnotic drive in his playing and "singing" that gave them the sound of tempestuous utterance.

TALE OF A HOLLYWOOD ORGY

Out of the many anecdotes of Antheil in his Hollywood days, I tell this one because it is "pure Antheil"; Georgie's fully orchestrated character is in it.

MacArthur, Herman Mankiewicz, and I were separately employed in the M-G-M Studio. Our work was piddling, our salaries enormous, and around us was the glamorous inner circle of movie-dom which in that time was something like the Third Heaven described by the Prophet Mohammed.

Geniuses crowded the corridors. The commissary at noon looked like Valhalla and the Court of Venus. Costumed beauties, from peasants to princesses; lovely "Extras" in vari-colored tights and bulging bodices gave off waves of perfume that almost anesthetized the males bowed over their bowls of noodle soup. And, always, a troop of secretaries also filled the scene. At Metro, in that time, secretaries were in the front lines of the studio's sexual activities; nearly all of them shirtwaist Lady Hamiltons of the type-writer.

I mention these details to indicate that we were no three desert hermits whom Antheil coaxed one evening into attending a performance of the ballet. He had written the music for one of the four dances that were on the bill.

I forget what Antheil's ballet was about. I remember that we watched it from the wings beside Georgie, and that MacArthur, Manky, and I were identically impressed by what we saw. Men rarely reveal such profound moods to each other, but our behavior made them obvious.

Antheil had introduced us into the world of the ballet. All the movie sirens and secretaries who were part of our daily scene became in our minds a wan and invalid group.

The twelve young ballerinas we had watched displaying their voluptuous muscles, leaping, whirling, and shooting out smiles, were more than females. Their almost nude bodies were clothed in art and draped with music.

We joined the ballerinas in their dressing rooms and watched them change from fairy-tale folk into almost human beings. And we looked on our friend Georgie with new eyes. We had been a little worried about his holding down his place in the movies. Music-writing jobs were, even in that booming time, not easy to land. But why should anyone want to stay in the movie world who had a standing in this world of ballet?

A few days later we called on Georgie and told him we wanted to give a party for his ballet troupe, omitting its four male dancers who, as often happens in that art, considered females diverting only as acrobats. We would hire a whole restaurant and the twelve ballerinas could eat, drink, and dance for us as long as they wished. Or we would be content to just sit among them, three for each of us, for there would be only MacArthur, Manky, Georgie, and I to pay them homage. We would also chip in and arrange for each of the ballerinas to find a fifty-dollar bill under her plate, as in the sybaritic days of Diamond Jim Brady.

Antheil was overjoyed.

"For next Sunday night," said our Georgie, "there's no performance on Sundays. The girls will be crazy happy to come. They were all very impressed with you."

On Sunday, 8 P.M., MacArthur, Mankiewicz, and I sat in our hired restaurant, "Little Hungary" on the Sunset Strip. We had payed in advance for twenty-four dinners and as many bottles of wine. And we had helped move a score of tables into the alley behind the cafe. There would be, thus, plenty of space for dancing. One long, flower-decked table for our ballerinas and ourselves remained on the premises.

At 8:30 P.M. the three of us began to worry over the continued absence of Antheil and the ballerinas.

"Musicians are bad about dates," said MacArthur. "Georgie may have forgotten the right evening."

We sat another half hour in the dismantled cafe, glowering at each other and threatening to go home to our wives. These ladies had nobly given us permission for our bacchanalian adventure. They had referred to it all week as our "orgy," and advised us not to drink too much, or sprain our muscles trying to compete with the ballerinas.

At 9 P.M. there was a banging on the locked entrance door. We heard Antheil's voice.

He came into the cafe, alone.

"Don't worry, everything has turned out wonderfully," Georgie beamed. "For a while I was really upset. You see, I forgot that the ballet finished its engagement last night, Saturday, and, of course, they all went off to San Francisco, for the opening tomorrow night. But, please, listen" — we had become inattentive — "it turned out marvelously. I've brought the greatest ballerina of all time, greater even than Pavlova. The Czar and his whole family were crazy about her. She used to dance for them in the Winter Palace outside of St. Petersburg. Diaghilev always said she's the greatest dancing genius ever produced by Russia."

A lean old lady in a red wig, weighing around eighty pounds, stepped out of Antheil's car. We were introduced to the greatest of Russian ballerinas. The name is lost in my head, possibly due to the shock of seeing her as a replacement for the twelve young Venuses now in San Francisco.

Georgie beamed on the wizened old lady in the red wig like an idolator. We all bowed properly over the ancient hand she extended.

"I didn't even know she was in this country," Georgie went on. "It was by luck I heard she was in a little hotel in Santa Monica. She loves watching the ocean."

"Oh yes, I love the ocean," the old lady smiled.

"Madam has agreed to dance for us," Georgie said. "I know all her music — *Petrouchka, Swan Lake, Giselle,* and so forth."

I remember Antheil at the cafe piano, banging away for what seemed hours. And an old lady in her late seventies dancing in the empty cafe. She wore ballet slippers and a long skirt that flew about her and exposed her wire-like underpinnings. A great deal of chiffon obscured her wrinkled face and bony shoulders. A streamer flapped wildly from her red wig, and she smiled as she danced and danced.

MacArthur, Manky, and I agreed to remain and eat three of the twenty-four dinners we had paid for. We agreed to sit and watch the ancient lady caper until she ran out of steam. We agreed also not to denounce Georgie for an imbecile, and for producing a fiasco of which our wives would be sure to make jokes for a long time.

We agreed to all this Spartan behavior because we didn't want to spoil Georgie's grand evening. Everything the three of us had hoped for, was present for Antheil — the wonder of the world of ballet.

Clouting the piano, Antheil looked with swooning eyes on the wispy old lady who danced. He saw a remembrance of beauty, he beheld the past and its loveliness. He sat, playing humbly (and loudly) for the greatest of all ballerinas.

Around midnight, MacArthur walked with some difficulty to the dance floor and bowed before the Czar's favorite in her red wig and swathing of chiffon.

"No, no, I am not tired," the ancient one squealed, as do Russian ladies of all ages, "I can dance more."

"You have danced enough," said MacArthur, "and very beautifully."

Manky and I bore him out by applauding. MacArthur led the fragile-looking old dancer to our flower-decked table. Despite her remarkable exertions, she wasn't even breathing hard.

"You will find a little present under each plate," MacArthur said to her.

Antheil watched the once greatest of ballerinas pick up the twelve fifty-dollar bills. She did it gracefully, as if it were part of a pretty game. She stuffed the bills into her blouse, that seemed to be empty of any other contents. Georgie cried out joyously:

"Just like it was in the days of the Czar, when you danced to Glazunov's music at the Winter Palace!"

And he played something stirring on the piano.

*   *   *

To sum up the genius of Antheil, here is a partial list of his activities, outside his constant activity of writing and playing music.

He wrote a number of books about himself and his adventures. They are the most readable volumes I have ever read from the pen of a musician.

He had a firm grip on endocrinology and wrote a number of important medical papers on that science for various periodicals.

He was an active criminologist and spent much time with

the Los Angeles police officials. He instructed them in certain glandular theories about crime and criminals. For instance, a murder marked by brutality and violence was most apt to be the deed of a hyperthyroidic glandular type. Since such types were lean, nervous, usually dark haired, thin lipped and bulbous eyed, the police could tell what the killer looked like. They could and did. Antheil was frequently congratulated by the Los Angeles police captains for having set them on a correct trail in a murder hunt.

One of Antheil's more uncanny talents was his ability to raid dusty warehouses and fish valuable "Old Masters" out of them. He could spot Italian and German old masters that had been painted over and thus reduced to worthless seeming canvases. Nearly always his "finds" were authenticated by his good friend Berenson in Rapallo, Italy. When Antheil died he left behind on his walls dozens of valuable paintings that he had bought for a song in secondhand shops and at obscure auctions.

Antheil was also a gifted engineer. He collaborated with movie star, Hedy Lamarr, on the invention of a new type of submarine, and secured a patent from Washington for its building. I have been told by Navy officials that, despite the later invention of the atomic powered submarine, the Antheil-Lamarr ship has many advantages to offer our underwater travelers.

And, finally, there was George Antheil, pianist member of an orchestra I assembled in Hollywood. A more discouraging group of musicians never toiled through a rehearsal.

Our ensemble included Harry Kurnitz, who owned a five-thousand-dollar fiddle. He played it with his left wrist flattened motionlessly against its neck. Harpo Marx, a champion harpist, played the clarinet. He was unable to read music and the clarinet part had to be whistled to him. Brother Groucho Marx attended several rehearsals as a guitarist. He was dismissed from my Symphonietta because no one was able to hear the feeble sounds of his instrument.

Kurnitz, who once had been a music critic, had provided the Symphonietta title, with my name included as its leader.

Groucho showed up at our next rehearsal with a full orchestra of his own. They were professional musicians, and their playing in an adjoining room drowned out our attempts to master Strauss' *The Emperor's Waltz*. We took Groucho back into our group, after he agreed to send his own ensemble packing.

Playwright Dwight Taylor, Director William Wyler, George Stoll, head of M-G-M's music department, author Everett Freeman and a half-dozen others whose names I have forgotten participated in our weekly rehearsals. With the exception of Stoll, they were all hopelessly butter-fingered instrumentalists. For weeks they played as if they were a pack of palsied deaf-mutes. They improved a little. Jack Benny and Benny Goodman joined the Symphonietta, but defected after a first rehearsal.

The worst of our lot was Charles Lederer who, mysteriously, owned a snare drum. Lederer was not only tone-deaf, along with most of his fellow orchestra members, but he was also time-deaf. He is the only human I have ever known who was unable to detect the one, two, three beat of a waltz.

We thought several times of replacing him, but his passion for playing the drum made him immune to insult and pleading. Antheil also spoke up for him. Charlie's inability to hit his drum at the right time fascinated our pianist.

"That's the sort of anti-rhythms I tried for in my *Ballet Mécanique*," said Georgie. "It's almost musically impossible to play the drum as Charlie plays it."

So Lederer continued in our rehearsals to throw our players into complete confusion by mis-beating the drum for *The Emperor's Waltz*. Antheil finally solved the problem. He moved Lederer to a spot beside him at the piano. Thus, while playing the piano, Georgie was able to indicate each drum beat with a thrust of his right hand.

After a summer of rehearsals, we mastered our sole number, *The Emperor's Waltz*. We were booked as the opening attraction of the Screen Writers' Guild's annual Prom or Hop. With our audience of literateurs sitting on the dance floor and listening in obvious amazement, we played *The Emperor's Waltz* through without boggle, and with all the instruments finishing at the same time.

The ballroom rang with the cheers of moviedom's scenarists, their wives and concubines. Having mastered no other piece, we responded to the cries for an encore by playing *The Emperor's Waltz* over again, with the same success that had marked our first performance of the number.

I leave George Antheil at the piano that night. Outside the windows of the ballroom glittered Los Angeles' tropical night sky, which receives almost no publicity. It was a beautiful sky. I can see its star-strewn vault beyond the windows; and our Georgie's face with a touch of moonlight on it. Our composer of symphonies, operas, cantatas, and concertos; our virtuoso who had stormed the concert halls of Europe, our friend Georgie sat that night playing the piano part of *The Emperor's Waltz* (and directing the Lederer drum beats) with his second expression on his face — the beam of pure happiness.

> *2711 Laurel Canyon*
> *Hollywood 46, Calif.*
> *November 6, 1944*

Dear Ben and Rose,

Boski and I would like to invite the two of you to dinner, here, some night. Do you come to town often? I tried to get in touch with you both a few weeks ago, but without success. I also wrote you a letter, but I guess you didn't get it. No matter, as the occasion about which I wrote is passed. But the desire to see you both still remains deep.

I am out of a job, at present, so, as per usual, I turn to musical composition. I have become a veritable factory of notes and music-paper filled to the last square inch. I earned some money with John Nesbitt, as a writer, but unfortunately had to buy this house as they were just about to sell it over our heads, and there was no other place to go.

So, to earn money, I am writing a book which I've sent one third to a big N.Y. publisher, and they pretend to be wildly enthusiastic about it. It's a book of adventures and life of G.A. Mebbe I'll make a killing with it, but more mebbe not. However.

Yes, I live in rapture, believe it or not. I am writing better music than ever; and now a whole lot of conductors all over the world are writing me. All over the world that still would consider music like mine, I mean. This includes London and Moscow.

My Fifth, which you heard part of, is now orchestrated. It is like a gigantic novel of today . . . a bigger canvas than the last. But, I still don't *know*, how good. I *think* it is the best. Klemperer, who was here the other night to dinner, and who is still extremely astute about matters musical, thinks it is a great symphony, and he is a hard hard hard guy to please.

Wot about Ben Hecht Symphonietta?

Anyway, we miss you. Now that the election's over. . . . ?

Devotedly,

GEORGE
ANTHEIL

610 West End Avenue
New York City, N.Y.

Dear Ben,

As far as playing the piano on the program is concerned, I can always do that. I think we are both agreed, however, that it should not be in the shape of complete pieces, but short examples of various music to the point, if such be necessary. I suppose there are a lot of things, directions, you could interview me about. As far as what's best for me — I think the best thing in the world for me is for me to appear on television with you, as your old friend, than have the Legion d'Honneur. Whatever you do or say will be O.K.

These are just some ideas which I am throwing at you in a relaxed way. For instance, when you have interviewed other types of artists, poets, etc., you have interviewed them from the standpoint that the viewing public are very interested in their innermost secrets of creation. The dopey who looks and listens takes this as a compliment from you personally "if Ben Hecht thinks I can digest and understand this, who am I to gainsay him"; in other words he feels good and "understands" whether he does or not. He comes out of the whole thing feeling, somehow, improved; and as the Number One Attraction in everybody's life is "Myself And How Can I Become More Beautiful, Intelligent, Attractive, Successful" this is not taking a great chance. (I think.)

So, to start at the hardest first: "In what direction, today, is so called serious music going?" My thesis: it is going in the direction of America. Why? Because, unlike Europe, we have not been robbed of ten to fifteen years of our development by a great war. Examples: when Hitler arrived on the scene in 1933, German music creation stopped, broke down altogether in 1936. Hitler allowed nothing but the most insiped Wagner-copying composers to remain on the scene. During 1933 to 1939 French composers also became frightened; and, as for Italy, or Spain, there was nothing, nothing. From 1939 to 1945 art development was completely suppressed in Europe, composing with it. From 1945 to 1950 we, over here, began to see something very extraordinary happen in Europe. The new German composers, who had never been interested Strawinsky and the Paris School, suddenly became extremely influenced by him; and the now top two or three German composers of

today come right out of this period—with Germanic over-
tones of their own of course, but definitely Strawinsky. The
French composers, who up to that moment had hated everything German, especially modern German, suddenly embraced Schonberg, Webern, the 12-tone School.

Ben Hecht: "What is 12 tone, Georgie?"

Georgie: (illustrating on the piano) "It is the *system* of
music which is discussed more today than any other; for
instance, here's the regular C Major scale, seven notes (playing C D E F G A B C) which ends on C, or the same tone,
eight notes—or an octave—higher. Most of the music of
the past has been written in that scale, in some other key
perhaps, or with slight variations of that scale, but that
scale nevertheless. THE TWELVE TONE SCALE is merely
the chromatic scale (playing the chromatic scale) but the
main idea of the twelve tone *system* is that once you hit any
note of that scale, you can't hit it again until you've sounded
in whatever order you please the other eleven."

Ben "Is there any advantage to this system, Georgie?"

Georgie. "The only advantage is that like cubism, or
abstractionism in painting, it makes everything sound aw-
fully modern. If you really keep the 12 tone system going,
you cannot write concords, and everything becomes dissonant. For instance, here's "Yankee Doodle" as it was
originally conceived, and here it is as a twelve tone system
piece (plays and illustrates; the 12 tone version is terribly
dissonant and scarcely recognizable—just about—as Yankee Doodle".)

Ben Hecht "Well let's get back to why you think music
creation is flowing in the direction of America? You were
saying that all modern German composers were composing
like Strawinsky after the war, and modern French were
composing like the Germans in dissonant 12 tone."

Georgie "They are doing their home work, catching up
on the ten to fifteen or even twenty years of development
which all Europe lost between 1933 and 1953. Most Ameri-

can composers went through their ultra rhythmic phrase or/ and ultra dissonant phrase during the early part of this period, and have made progress since, so that, in my opinion, as a "school" we are at least ten years ahead of Europe, today. I don't know whether that applies to writers or painters: I suspect that we're either tied, or ahead of them here, too. Let's face it, the European artist has had ten to fifteen years cut right out of his life. Excepting Britten, in England, I do not really see talents in Europe comparable to our Leonard Bernstein, Menotti, Barber, and a whole slew of younger composers like Benny Lees . . . These men are doing *something new*.

Ben Hecht: "Something new — modern — is something that's really new, you mean, not assembly-line modern"

Georgie "12 tone system is an old story for me; it was my mother's milk. When I was 24 years old, I wrote my first work which was practically in this system throughout. For me to write exactly like that, today, would be to attempt a youthful nostalgia which I could never recapture because it belongs to some part of me long ago disappeared. (Plays example of Ballet Mecanique) I can teach a seven year old child how to write in 12 tone, and it will always sound "modern", the same as if one methodically teaches the same child how to be a cubist painter. The Strawinsky system of using old harmonic devices, mostly, but with new rhythmic upserstructure, is I think more artistic. (Illustrates Yankee Doodle as a Strawinsky composition.) The frank truth of the whole matter is, everything they are doing in Europe today SOUNDS OLD FASHIONED TO ME. De-mode modernism. Just before he died I think that one of the leaders of the 12 tone system thought so too — in any case he was a real artist and not the follower of a system; he was Arnold Schonberg. We saw him quite often during the last years of his life.

Ben Hecht "With your anti 12 tone views, I wonder that he let you into the house."

G.A. "It was all a mistake. Som[e]where along in 1946 I became very angry with the blind followers of Strawinsky, and the blind followers of Schonberg, and I prepared a lecture against both of them. It was a very vitrolic denunciation — I wouldn't do such a thing today, being by no means as sure of my then-arguments today. But, as I commenced my anti-Strawinsky-Schonberg lecture, I saw Mr. Schonberg in the front row. So I switched my lecture around and started attacking Strawinsky first. Schonberg glowed, kept nodding his head in agreement with me; he even smiled. After that I didn't have the nerve to go on. I improvised the rest of the lecture, and Schonberg came up, and we became friends. I've never felt so queezy about anything, but it did show me one thing: Schonberg wasn't in agreement with his fanatical followers either. "A system like the 12 tone, is merely there to be hel[p]ful" he once told me. "Once it becomes a bondage, it becomes something to cast off." Spoken like the true artist he was.

(etc. etc. the American supremacy in creative music can be further developed; this is just an idea; it would also get me to play the piano.)

Or Ben, you could just ask me what I'm doing now: and I could plunge into my doings which, as you know, are multitudinous as ever. A musical, a new musical, a Christmas opera: this also gives opportunity to play.

Anecdotes: you once told me that the reason I was hired by you at first was that Oscar Levant concked out on you over at Astoria, and you were looking for a composer tough enough to stand the situation. You thought of me as you remembered my episode in Budapest, where I took out a revolver and put it on the piano, telling the attendants to "lock the doors". (This actually happened; it was when I was fed up on the rioting in the cities I had previously played in.) One of my proudest anecdotes is when I singlehandedly defied Hitler & Co. It was in Munich, in 1923, and I was supposed to give a piano recital of French, English and

American music. An anonymous letter came into my concert agency, saying that if I played such a concert in Munich, the Hall would be bombed. I asked, was it serious? The agency said yes, for the police had traced it to the Hitler mob, then hatching the Nazi movement; they were capable of actually bombing the hall. I had read about Hitler, despised him, said "I will give the concert anyhow", and I did, although American[s] in Munich of that date attempted to dissuade me. The notices were very good, too, although several critics said that I played a little nervously in the first number. The budding Hitler was outbluffed. My Munich was a little different from that of Chamberlain's some years later. . . .

My God, I have so many anecdotes that I wouldn't be able to put them all down here, unless you think that this is the angle . . . I first met Boris Morros on the back of an elephant in the ball park at Nyack, Charlie MacArthur and I were friends in Hollywood in the early days of mine, there, and I saw a good deal of him; etc. etc. Perhaps another angle is this: how does a serious composer make a living . . . ? A lot of people might like to know the practical side . . . in short, to embrace the life of a composer of serious music (or any serious art) is tantamount to embracing the life of a pirate, a con-man, a life of high adventure, morally high only because one never gives in on the quality — for whatever it is intended. The Greeks were the world's most artistic people because they applied art to everything, their utensils, their life, everything. It was not beneath their greatest sculptors to do scroll-work. . . .

Love,
GEORGE

8161 Laurel View Dr.
Hollywood 46, Calif.
April 1, 1957

Dear Ben,

Believe it or not, this is the first opportunity I've had since I last saw you face to face, to write. I have to make some explanations, inasmuch as there were so many matters pending. I wanted to thank Rose for her lovely record and particularly, for her lovely letter. I wanted to record the song I wrote for her — I have the singer, finally. I wanted to record the piano pieces for Jenny. I wanted to record the love themes for David Selznick. And send all of them to the persons for whom they are intended.

Directly after I last saw you at the Beverly Hills, however, they came down on me for a picture score I had contracted for at Columbia months before; it was during our busy season (December-January-February) and all of my orchestrators were busy, so I not only had to compose all of the 55 minute score, but orchestrate it as well, as well as supervise its recording. On top of that a big opportunity of C.B.S.T.V. arrived; and I sat down and wrote 20 more minutes for large orchestra. Then, with one day's rest in-between, Stanley Kramer delivered the PRIDE AND THE PASSION to me, which has a two hour score. So I sat down and wrote that; the start was just a little over a month ago. Fortunately, being past tax date, I could get all of my regular assistants (who are all tops in their line, orchestra-contractor, music cutter, conductor, and orchestrators) so it hasn't quite been the grind that the Columbia picture was. I finished two days ago with the final composition — a necessity because the copyists must have it several days ahead of the recording in order to get out the parts. We start recording tomorrow, Tuesday, April 2. I feel like the pilot of one of those airplanes they send into a hurricane to find its center and direction. I am in dead-center, the middle of a great calm, with a hugh $6,000,000 hurricane raging all about me; and I must fly back, through it, to reach safty. We're going to have a tumultuous week of recording ahead. But Stanley Kramer seems on my side. I don't know whether you know him; but he is a rather dry guy who almost never says "thank you" or "I like it" whenever you do something for him; it isn't that he is ungrateful, but he just isn't that sort of guy. After I played the piano score for him the other day he said "I think it is a great score, just what I wanted" and warmly shook my hand. And, above all, looked relieved. He has a lot at stake. We're hoping for the best; but things can always go askew at recordings, no matter how well planned. Nowadays I and my crew usually keep these things down to a minimum. This will be 7/8ths of the picture score; Stanley still had to shoot a few scenes yesterday; but these need scoring of a small kind; and I can do it in another recording in two weeks, perhaps within one day. In the meantime they want to dub; apparently they have a pressure preview or release date in mind, in June I think.

In short, I just haven't had time to breath(e); this, in the middle of the hurricane center, is my first chance, and I am using one of the first moments of it to write to you. Maia tells me that rumor has it that you are in Italy; accordingly I am sending this to Nyack, but putting enough postage on it for overseas, just in case you are not there. I knew, last time I saw you, that you were longing to go abroad.

Regarding David Selznick, we've been reading that he has been having his troubles; therefore, frankly, even though I had had the time to recompose my material more in line with what we discussed when you last heard it on the piano, I would have been a little afraid to send him the recordings during this period. However, just as soon as I get out of this Kramer thing, I'm going to get at it — I've composed some new material meanwhile which I personally think is just what he wants and needs, simple, melodically strong and retainable, still capable of great passionate development while being naively heartwarming and heart-breaking with an Italian inflection. Somewhere around the middle or end of this month I am going to send it to him anyway, just on the chance.

Well, Ben, this brings you up to date and explains, I hope, my tardiness. I am also going to write to Rose, to whom I owe a letter. This is the first time in many weeks I've taken the cover from the typewriter. But it is wonderful to write to you first. I hope you're having a hell of a good time.

In afterstudy we pinpointed your primitive as definitely belonging to the Frankfurter school, or the school of Grune-wald. It is not by the Master, but is a fine example of his school. It is worth about $3,500, or ten times what you paid for it. I do hope you like it still for, as soon as I knew you liked Grunewald so much I determined that the first time I came across anything of his school I'd either buy it myself for you, or put you wise to it. The period around which I found it, however, is usually my financially low period, the period during which I am waiting for the pictures I've contracted for, and which will not be paid for until the scores are delivered.

Prestudy, now being made by top authorities in Italy, seem to indicate that my 50" by 10" battle study IS *related* to the lost cartoon by Michaelangelo, which can either mean that he sketched it, or a pupil (but his pupils were Tintoretto, etc!) I can now say that it is a sketch of this lost cartoon, of the school of Michaelangelo; but I may be able to do better with the passing of time. I have bought no new pictures since my Van Der Weyden school primi-tive — I've been too busy. But I have the nucleous of a nice little collection, all good pictures by first class masters. Oh yes, I forgot, I have the restored Piazzetta home, now. He predates, and influenced Tiepolo; it's a lovely picture.

The museum, here, now woos me, has its eye on the Van Der Weyden, the Piazzeta, and the Michaelangelo school. They are all, really, museum pieces. It's a lot of fun, and relaxing.

My new opera, "Venus In Africa" will be premiered in late May; rehearsals, I understand, are already under way. The Cabeza De Vaca Cantata will not come out until next season. Love.

GEORGE

About MacArthur

My friendships with the men in these pages were a full half of my life, as masculine friendships are to most men.

A loving woman who dies or turns her back usually liberates a man's heart to love another woman. This is not true about a vanished male friend. His death does not liberate; it lessens. Matthew Arnold in his poem "Thyrsis" wrote of the death of his friend Arthur Hugh Clough, "The bloom is gone, and with the bloom go I."

My friends who died took with them part of my bloom. I felt more lessened than mournful. The world grew smaller with their leaving.

Of these buried ones, the most related to me was Charles MacArthur. I would like to write of MacArthur what I once felt about him, but that is difficult. Friendship dies with a dead friend. Therein lies one's lessening.

In fact, as you grow older you begin to feel victimized by dead friends. They become names in which much of yourself is locked away, and unusable.

You don't blame them, but you blame something of which they were a deceptive part — mortality. You begin to look on mortality as a practical joke which, with their aid, took you in for a long time. Whoever thought in these sunny years that the table would be vacant, the room empty?

Of my friend MacArthur I have left an album of memory photographs, forty years of them; pictures full of mysterious poses. They grin and stare like a code to be deciphered. Was that Charlie? How did he happen to be wearing a chef's hat? Was it in Charleston or San Francisco that he played that clarinet? Since he never danced, how does he happen to be dancing a sensuous tango in a Mexico City ballroom? And where the devil did he dress up in a robe of white bed sheets with a hangman's noose around his neck?

There are scores of such pictures. Clues to life or, as Charlie's favorite poet, Henry W. Longfellow, put it, "footprints on the sands of time." I never fully understood MacArthur's enthusiasm for Longfellow. It had more to do with the bard's sonorous name and flowing whiskers than with his poetry. It had to do also with what I fancy as the source of most of my friend's secrets — his boyhood.

It was Longfellow who inspired MacArthur to one of his most grandiose dreams. In the first years of his exile in New York (from Arcadian Chicago) MacArthur took a flier in the cemetery business. He undertook, for a percentage of the profits, to promote a New Jersey burial ground into a sort of American Westminster Abby to which the bodies of famous Americans would be shipped and grandly reinterred.

Charlie's first bid was for the body of Henry Wadsworth Longfellow, at rest in Boston soil. Charlie went to Boston and convinced its mayor that Longfellow's body should lead the march of the nation's great corpses to the New Jersey Valhalla.

But there was a hitch. Boston's Brahmins raised a ruckus against the kidnaping of their finest and noblest poet. Press and pulpit denounced the proposed highjacking of their illustrious dead. The mayor bowed to the storm.

Charlie's last gesture in behalf of his Valhalla was a curt telegram to Boston's two-faced mayor. It read: ROLL THEM BONES.

Such are the pictures of the young MacArthur that remain in my mind, bright with the subject's remarkable charm and good looks. But chiefly, they have a humorous air. They make me smile when I look at them. They seem like a photographer's report of a carnival.

*   *   *

MacArthur and I became friends in our Chicago teens. Charlie worked on morning newspapers, the *Tribune* and the *Examiner;* I on afternoon papers, the *Journal* and the *Daily News.* The stories we covered were part of our friendship. They remained a world out of which neither of us entirely emerged. We interviewed thieves, swindlers, murderers, lunatics, fire bugs, bigamists, gangsters, and innumerable sobbing ladies who had taken successful potshots at their married lovers.

For all such evil-doers Charlie had a sort of collector's enthusiasm. Crime and disaster allured him, socially. Hangings, death beds, 4–11 fires, protracted gun battles between cops and loonies, mysterious corpses popping out of river and swamp, courtrooms and jail cells loud with deviltries, were a sort of picnic ground for MacArthur. For me, also.

We never discussed our attitudes. Sharing them was enough. Charlie's attitudes? Blithe is one word for them. But there was a complexity under his pleased look at the life around him. The complexity grew in the years that followed. What this out-of-sight MacArthur was, I never found out. I knew only that secrets were in him, like a wind blowing, threatening to tip him over.

Charlie, from the beginning, had a poet's infatuation with death. It was a sort of private moonlight in which he walked around. Though he seemed as unreligious as a Hottentot, he kept an eye out for God, and conducted throughout his life a love affair with his Maker that was nobody's business.

There was also a wildness in Charlie, but it was well policed. It never disturbed the conventionalities of his mind. It caused him to break neither laws nor idols, but he had to feed the daemon in him a great deal of liquor to keep it in line.

It was this wild streak that made him feel at home amid calamities, all except one — the death of his bright and sweet daughter, Mary. The torment of her young dying remained with him to his last hour.

External troubles such as wars and revolutions allured him all his life as parties might a playboy. In his teens Charlie enlisted in the U. S. Army when it went chasing Pancho Villa in Mexico. Pancho was never caught. On the other hand our armed forces suffered one casualty. A Chicagoan, Sammy Meisenberg, was fatally shot during the battle of Vera Cruz.

Charlie returned from his first military adventures with anecdotes that bedazzled us stay-at-homes. He had served in Colonel Milton Foreman's Illinois militia. To the end of his days, Colonel Foreman would blanch at the mention of MacArthur's name.

I'll record of Charlie's Mexican Campaign only such honest items as that he set rivers to running up hill, filled the campsites with swooning señoritas, and would have caught Pancho Villa singlehanded, himself, if only Colonel Foreman had let him.

In 1915 Charlie hied himself off to Canada to enlist in its Black Watch regiment that was heading for the German battle front. He was thwarted, despite the fact that he had brought his own uniform along, and was forced to wait until President Wilson gave the go-ahead for the U.S. troops. Whereupon Charlie hopped off for the Argonne and Cantigny as a member of Battery F of the 149th Field Artillery, 42nd (Rainbow) Division.

He curried the artillery horses and lifted cannon shells in a dozen gory battles.

After our side won the war (that was fought to put an end to all militarism and "Power Politics") Charlie wrote a book about his Battery F pals. It was titled *A Bug's Eye View of the War*. It is possibly the only happy, delighted book ever written by a soldier about bloody and deadly

battles in which he fought. It offered no ideas of any kind
concerning the causes or patriotic objectives of the conflict.

What could there be delightful and happy in a war that
killed and crippled some four million men? Charlie Mac-
Arthur. And not Charlie alone. Battery F was his claque
and court. They picnicked with him amid shot and shell.
An air of high-jinks surrounded even their red-hot cannon.
In his book, MacArthur mourns briefly the buddies who
were killed. But the party goes on, through French villages,
forced marches and battlefields.

The officers of the 149th Regiment of the Rainbow Division came to look on Battery F with bafflement. It seemed
to be fighting a different war than the rest of the American
Expeditionary Forces. There was the matter of its oriental
ritual. Its privates saluted respectfully any sergeant, lieutenant, or captain who addressed them. But the officers were
reduced to glaring confusedly at a superior type of discipline practiced by Battery F's members. I'll let Charlie tell
it, again.

"Our battery," Charlie used to tell at postwar dinner
tables, "got a little bored with saluting its officers as was
demanded by the rules of war. So we cooked up a plan to
improve our own social standing without disturbing this
army caste system. Every morning at breakfast we elected
a Caliph from our lowly midst. Only privates, in fact, were
eligible for this supreme honor.

"And for the rest of the day every private addressing his
Caliph had to bow low two times and begin each conversation with the august words, 'O Commander of the Faithful,
is it true that, etc.' It made our officers seem small potatoes
when you saw us privates constantly salaaming to a fellow
private and using such high-flown language."

The thirty-two surviving members of Battery F chipped
in for the private publication of *A Bug's Eye View of the
War*. They were eager to have their good times preserved

in print. And who but "Bugs" MacArthur, their favorite
Caliph, could do it justice?

Soon after the souvenir book appeared, one of Charlie's
editors, Joseph Medill Patterson, ran it as a serial in his
Liberty Magazine, and the nation saluted Battery F with a
loving grin. One of the oddities of Charlie's book is his
almost total absence from its pages. He wrote of others.

"Bugs" was Charlie's nickname in his Chicago days.
During his courtship of her, Helen Hayes gave him another.
She called him Charlie Macabre.

There were two songs Charlie used to sing in the twilight
when he sat in a room, remembering happy days. One was,

> *"My Mother called me to her dying bedside*
> *And these were the words that she said —*
> *'You'll be in trouble before you're dead, poor boy,*
> *You'll be in trouble before you're dead.*

The other was,

> *"She's gone, let her go, God bless her,*
> *For she never belonged to me.*
> *She can lard ass her way through the A.E.F.,*
> *But she'll never find a sucker like me."*

Too old to enlist as a private in World War II, Mac-
Arthur in 1942 reluctantly accepted a commission in the
rank of lieutenant colonel. But his heart was with his memories — in the rank and file of soldiering. He was as unique
a colonel as ever appeared on a battlefield or took part as a
hitchhiker in bombing raids. His letters from the front were
full of the same blitheness that had marked his newspaper
reporter accounts of crooks and bawds and minor local
shooting matches.

Despite Charlie's indignant statements that he was "in
the pink," an ulcer, kidney trouble, and an eye cataract dis-
qualified him from the Korean battlefields. Charlie had to
lighten his ennui as a civilian by scurrying off in airplanes

to Europe, Africa, and Asia. He was never the tourist in quest of new sights. He darted about the planet looking for "lively doings" — his favorite phrase. He usually found them.

I traveled occasionally with Charlie, and met the poltergeist world through which he gallivanted. We collided in Central America and in Mexico with revolutions, assassinations, firing squads, and other perils. Everybody seemed to be shooting at us — Zapatistas, government troops and, occasionally, individuals who had taken offense at insults of which we were innocent.

Charlie called the trip to Mexico, which we barely survived, "a fine vacation."

*   *   *

Among the Chicago pictures that linger are Charlie's fist fights. The set-tos were usually climaxes of religious arguments. In his cups, Charlie was touchy about scurrilous references to Christ or the Apostle Paul. Charlie's father had been an Evangelist in Nyack, New York, on whose riverbank Charlie and I both settled in our separate homes in the late '20s. Evangelist MacArthur had tried to beat the Devil out of his four sons in their boyhood, using a vinegar-soaked strap for his purpose. The self-ordained Reverend MacArthur, a rhapsodic Scott with a Vandyke, was not entirely successful. But he left his mark in his favorite son. In the years that followed, Charlie stood at Armageddon in many a barroom and battled for the Lord.

I never saw a fist fighter, in or out of the ring, quite like Charlie. He seemed to grow calmer during a slugging match. His expression, during a fight, was that of a man oddly amused. He would stand with his fists hanging at his side, waiting for his antagonist to come within range. Fists walloping his face seemed to make no impression on him. His pleased look remained. He struck rarely more than

one or two blows in combat. They usually laid low his
opponent, or discouraged his further efforts.

Charlie's fists continued to swing in Hollywood. Of his
successful bouts, I remember fondly the one with the movie
star, Jack Gilbert. Jack had been pestering a young
woman, being too drunk to notice she was going to become
a mother in a few weeks. Charlie picked up the movie star in
his arms and carried him off to a bedroom. Here he removed Jack's shoes and started undoing his tie. Jack, who
was proud of his boxing talent, hung a left hook on the
preoccupied Charlie's chin. He followed it with a right clout
to Charlie's jaw, and Charlie continued to undo the man's
tie.

"Now be a good lad," Charlie said, "lie down, say your
prayers and go to sleep."

He had struck no return blow, yet I never saw a man
more defeated than movie star Gilbert, staring up at his
smiling friend, MacArthur.

Charlie always returned from his foreign tours with
sprightly anecdotes. He brought them back as tourists come
home with souvenirs.

"I ran into Ernest Hemingway in a French village," said
Charlie. "After a few drinks in his house, the great author
insisted on us having a fight in his back yard. There was
no way of getting out of it, except if I took to my heels."

"Did you lick him?" I asked.

"No," said Charlie, "I had to put on boxing gloves. Ernest
sneered at bare-handed fighting. He said it was vulgar and
unscientific. We fought for quite a while. Ernest kept poking
me in the face with those padded gloves. I tried socking
him several times but the gloves slowed me up."

"Anybody get knocked out?" I asked.

"No," said Charlie, "but Ernest can hit hard, despite his
prancing around. When he announced suddenly that the
fight was over, because he never went more than three
rounds, I was glad to hear it."

*   *   *

Charlie came to New York in the mid '20s, and for the next fifteen years Charlie MacArthur was a legendary figure in the metropolis. Its elite fell all over one another trying to bag Charlie MacArthur as a dinner guest. In a city so full of personalities that nearly every hotel lobby looked like a Hall of Fame, Charlie stood out as he had in Chicago and on the Western Front.

I remember Charlie's popularity as one of the town's top phenomena. There were fine tales in that time of George S. Kaufman's wit, Alexander Woollcott's merry fi-fo-fumming, of Heywood Broun's spirituality, Dorothy Parker's fire-cracker repartée, Robert Benchley's jollity, Otto H. Kahn's Xanadu haven for artists, Horace Liveright's open pocket-book for book writers; of George Gershwin's persistent piano playing, Oscar Levant's hilarious insults, Ring Lardner's stoical liquor consumption, Innkeeper Frank Case's collection of actors' and authors' IOUs; of gay gatherings around Fanny Brice, Bea Lillie, Neysa McMein, Tommy Hitchcock, Jock Witney, Herbert Bayard Swope, etcetera. But when at last (O Saki) Charlie passed among the guests, star scattered in the grass, the tale of the MacArthur allure was at the top of the town's legends.

It sounded as brightly in London and Paris. And in Hollywood, in the time when its first swimming pools and Sindbad Studios swarmed with the world's most exotic personnel. In the '30s, the movie bosses, assembled in their creative conferences, kept saying, "Let's make the hero of this picture a real MacArthur. You know what I mean?"

I knew what they meant — a dashing, mysterious fellow, cool as a cucumber but exciting as hell. The secret of Charlie's popularity lay somewhere in that description.

My friend was a disturber of the peace, not in his actions or words, but himself. He was not wag or artist but something happening—an event of a man. Among ornate guests and famous talents chirping the evening away, MacArthur was as diverting as a jail break. He ravished no debutantes, punched no celebrated noses, and refused stoutly to join in parlor games or raise his voice in group singing.

Yet women felt immoral in his presence. Men felt a lift of adventure. And all listened to Charlie's stories. Never was there more literature tossed out of a window. Corpses, rogues and nymphomaniacs stepped out of Charlie's memories. Lamas, grand duchesses, pickpockets, opera stars, pyromaniacs, gangsters, and moonshooters all up and down the globe pranced about again in his anecdotes.

F. Scott Fitzgerald wrote to Charlie's wife, Helen, "There are some people who are better than artists, who are works of art, themselves—like Charlie."

And so he was in his legendary years when all his genius was content to entertain a porch full of beaming strangers. Georg Brandes wrote, "He who writes in Danish writes on water." My friend Charlie did his finest writing on thin air.

Not entirely. He spun his tales also for his bride, Helen. His "lively doings," from boyhood to his death filled her life. He wrote, also, some fine plays and movies for a larger audience.

*   *   ●

MacArthur and I began writing plays together in the mid '20s. Our first play was titled *The Moonshooter*. We wrote it during a summer together in Woodstock, New York. We were both broke. J. P. McEvoy, another Chicago exile, had loaned me and Rose his woodland house. Charlie's love, actress Helen Hayes, was touring in a play, and he had to pause in his courtship and moon around until her return. Rose was with me, managing somehow to keep us all fed.

without money. Her chief duty, however, was listening to
our rival anecdotes.

We were satisfied with this audience of one. (I was never
to find a better one.) But Rose took to writing a novel,
hiding in the woods with her pencils and paper. Charlie
and I, fed up with each other's oft told tales, went to work
inventing a new one in *The Moonshooter.*

We borrowed money (from somewhere) for a journey to
Sam H. Harris's house in Long Island. The amiable, half-
deaf Mr. Harris was one of Broadway's leading play producers. I read our play to him at the top of my voice.
When I finished, Mr. Harris embraced us as a pair of fine
comedy playwrights. He had heard hardly half the play,
but he liked us. He promised us a production as soon as
we finished some rewrite of the work.

"I don't think you ought to kill a hero off in a comedy,"
Sam said. "I may be wrong, but I have that feeling."

"It's a comic death," said Charlie.

Sam shook his head stubbornly. "I don't think an audience is going to laugh much at a dead man," he said. "Especially a fine fella like you boys have written."

We didn't argue, but drank more of Sam's liquor. On
the train to New York, we decided to let our hero, whose
name was Enoch, die as we had written.

Enoch had rescued a woman murderess from her death
cell and whisked her to the Honduras. Here he had become
involved in a war between the Honduras Republic and the
British Empire. As he was ordering his raggedy troops to
"man the coffee warehouse" against the approaching British Navy, a California sheriff appeared, demanding the person of the murderess (I forget her name) rescued by
Enoch. She was a rather irritating and righteous young
woman, but Enoch, being Enoch, refused to surrender her.
Whereupon the California sheriff opened fire. A bullet sent
Enoch into his death scene.

Looking bewilderedly at his little scarecrow army and at

the daft lady whom he had gallantly rescued from the gallows, our wounded Enoch sighed and said, "I didn't mean to die like this." And died.

We were sure a second, louder, reading of the play would convince Sam we had done right by Enoch. But somewhere during that summer night we lost our play manuscript. We had taken turns typing it. As former newspapermen, we typed without thought of carbon copies.

Possibly *The Moonshooter* disappeared while we sat on a Broadway curbing till dawn, trying to convince our friend Harold Ross, of the bifurcated teeth and Ozark haircut, that he was not designed to run the stylish literary magazine *The New Yorker,* for which he was foolishly trying to raise money.

"With your talent for laughing like a hyena at bum jokes," said Charlie, "you would be better off running 'Jim-Jam-Jems.'"

When the three of us fell to rest in the Astor Hotel, *The Moonshooter* had vanished. I remember it as the best work Charlie and I did together.

Luckily, we hung on to our ensuing manuscripts: *The Front Page, Twentieth Century, Jumbo* for the theater; *The Scoundrel, Gunga Din, Crime Without Passion, Wuthering Heights,* and a dozen other movie scenarios.

* * *

In our twenty years of off-and-on collaboration there was never any debate between us. We worked without ego as if we were playing a game, the rule of which was, "whoever objects, wins." We argued about everything on earth except a line of dialogue or a plot turn. A shake of the head was sufficient rebuttal by either of us.

I sat, pencil in hand, with a lap board for a desk. Charlie usually leaned out of my Nyack window and studied the bird life in a nearby maple tree, or the symmetrical

ripples on the nearby Hudson River. In winter, he fussed
with the fire logs as we composed, or drew cartoons of
cannibals frying missionaries.

I wrote more of the dialogue and came up with more of
the plot turns, but it was Charlie who was more the playwright. He loved the stage more. It was a place of all importance to him. A wrong speech, a contrived situation made
his soul wince. He seemed to know the unseen road on
which we were embarked.

Comedy was our mutual enthusiasm. We had the same
eye and ear for the innocent oddities of humans. So alike
were our tastes and inventiveness that I have seldom been
able to tell, after a work was done, which lines he or I
had written.

Why collaborate when you can do a work by yourself?
We had different reasons. Mine was that I needed somebody else's love for the stage as a stimulant. The success the
theatre had to offer appealed to me less than the satisfac-
tions I found in writing books.

It was otherwise with Charlie. The stage was his homeland. But he lacked the discipline for lone expression. He
needed a monitor to hold him to a task, however much he
loved it.

Our only separate attitudes as playwrights was our reac-
tion to critics, derogatory ones. Charlie concealed his hurt,
and hurt it is when the critic commandos of the press storm
the stage and wipe out your play. This befell us twice on
adaptations of other writers' plays — *Swan Song* and *Ladies
and Gentlemen.*

That they were somewhat wobbly offerings did not lessen
the burn of injustice we felt. Playwrights are more given to
rages and depressions over bad reviews than are book
writers. Perhaps because there is more at stake, financially.
An adverse book review in the press leaves your book
alive. However impudent its critics, it remains on your shelf,
and you can fancy it a triumphant answer to its detractors.

And quote Schopenhauer a bit smugly: "When a book and a head come into contact, and one of them sounds hollow — is it always the book?" Besides, who ever dreams of getting rich out of writing a book?

The playwright is another story. He dreams of bonanza royalties and movie sales. And his dreams and play are both clumsily destroyed by unpleased critics. As Kierkegaard wrote, "It is like being trampled to death by geese."

There was a favorable balance of praise for MacArthur's output. His drama *Lulu Belle,* written with Edward Sheldon, and most of his collaborations with me were nicely welcomed. They added another dimension to his popularity, his charm and intactness.

Then why is it with all this victory and laughter that was MacArthur do I hear the sound of pain and sadness around his name? Is it because he changed too much; because in his last years age, alcohol and disease looted him of looks and talent? Yes, Charlie seemed to have lost or drunk away all but one of his many gifts. His courage remained.

He could grin at his fingers swollen to the size of bananas, at the black patch that covered his bum eye, at the crooked cane that helped him shuffle slowly down his last streets. Grin even at the slurred words in his talk, at the fumble for memory.

But why remember a garden in winter, a man in pain? Forget it, Charlie. You had a fancy look in a cluttered world. None fancier, none kindlier, none more devil-may-care. The look that made fat Alec Woollcott coo over the radio, "What a perfect world this would be were it peopled only with Charlie MacArthurs."

During our long friendship, our lives frequently went off in different directions. We pursued our ways in totally different worlds. Yet such divorces never affected our relationship. We knew each other as if there had been no interruption. It was a mutual identity that I never quite understood.

When I stood in the funeral parlor and spoke to the mourners of the Charles MacArthur we were taking to his grave, I felt a bewilderment that almost silenced me. I wondered which of us was stretched out in the flower-heaped coffin.

*   *   *

Dear Ben,

The loud controversy on "Oversold" has been amicably settled by the addition in the by-line of Lloyd's full name and (I hope) his address. I'm sorry you were dragged into it after your lovingkindness in presenting me to the pope.

I told you why I took the position I did. The first story I considered to be collaberation. The second was a burlesque on the first situation of the first story, followed by plot detail all my own; and the old arrangement had gone by the board.

I do not think the story as it now stands can fairly be called collaboration, in any sense of the word. I wrote to Mencken merely to avoid the embarrassment of defending myself from intimations of plagiarism. I am writing you for the same reason. Lloyd's statements are hallucinations of the Devil, as demonstrated by the fact that his only complaint to me is that the story represents the sacreligious mutilation of a serious situation, which otherwise would have been the basis of a Great Book, on which he has pondered for two years.

Unconsciously, I am afraid, he had led you to think I haven't acted quite rightly in the matter. Beyond assuring you that I have, I will never mention it to you again.

You are batting 999 on the Back Page [of the News]. Will you have meat and potatoes with me Friday noon, or any

other noon. Call me at 11 if you will. Sup. 2300. I have a
Back Page story for you.

Yours in Xt,

MacArthur

Hotel Tamanaco
Caracas, Venezuela
Saturday

Dear Ben,

A fellow passenger on this bumboat just told me that
Walter Howey had died a few days back — a happy end, I
thought, for all that had befallen him since January. He
had broken his back a couple of years ago and was still in
a semi-cast when a runaway taxi climbed a sidewalk to
re-break it and shatter ten ribs besides. Pneumonia followed. One lung filled up and the other was half filled
when his young and really dedicated wife turned her face
to the wall, said "oh, my poor Wallie" and gave up the
ghost. She had been suffering from some tricky post-opera-
tive thyroid trouble and the shock was enough. When
Walter came to he learned that the funeral had been the
day before. It was all like the Book of Job.

I had been in touch with some of the boys up in Boston
and went up there as soon as he was able to see anyone.
Events had made him a little boy again. I meant to stay a
half an hour but he kept me all afternoon. After he broke
his back the first time I had sent him a watch with "To
the best newspaper man I know" on it and he was showing
it to visitors, calling us his detractors, meanwhile spinning
wonderful tales of the past. He had many fond memories
of Gene. Tell him, or send him this, because I haven't his
daffy address on board.

But the one thing on our old hero's mind was Gloria. He
was full of memories of how she stole his sox to keep him
from wearing them a second day and other loving minutae.
He planned to go from the hospital to their bed and some-

how find her there. There were a few unconscious tears through this, but mostly smiles. So I think when he got home and back in that bed she must have whispered to him in his sleep. (That's how he died, in his sleep) I called him until we left New York on the 19th. By that time his thoughts were centering more on their boy, Walter — no, *William* Randolph Howey, aged 16, who bolted the family circle to become a newspaper reporter (minus Walter's aid) after the old man was safely on his back the first time. He told me of his plan to bring him up as a memorial to Gloria. I hope it works out. I hear the kid is difficult, but who isn't at 16? His bolting sounded spirited.

This trip (mainly for *our* 16 year old) is about as I expected, paper hats, etc., although a paranoiac wife embarrassed her husband tonight by popping out of a port hole. It seems she suspected him of something. She was in her climacteric, they say. So am I, but my ulcer cards are proving useful, and I remain calm.

Lucy Kroll carried her notion of a book to the point of putting a tape recorder on board, plus two dozen reels of tape. Fortunately it calls for AC current. The ship uses DC.

That's all that's happened in the last ten days at sea. Only two items of interest have sifted through the ship's radio. McCarthy was demoted and Audrey Hepburn won an Oscar.

For the rest, due to Walter's going, I feel with Lancelot that "the good old times are dead" or dying.

Jim won the ship's ping pong contest. He doesn't *want* to be called Jamie anymore, and is chasing a blonde my size. Time sure flies.

Sunburned salutes to all.

CHARLIE

ABOUT ARTISTS

Artists are often the most bitter and gloomy of people.

Socrates wrote, "Life is a terrible thing." He considered it a disease. He commissioned his friend Crito to sacrifice a rooster after his death — as a thanks offering for his deliverance.

"Man," wrote Pascal, "is an incomprehensible monster."

Lord Byron wrote, "Man is a two-legged reptile, crafty and venomous."

Goethe wrote, "There is no need to visit a madhouse to find lunatics. So monstrous are our illusions, frenzies, hallucinations afloat in the world, that I sometimes wonder whether our planet is the asylum of the universe for disordered minds."

Dostoevsky wrote, "Is it not possible to eat me up without insisting that I sing the praises of my devourer?"

Lord Russell wrote, "human life, its growth, its hopes, fears, loves, etcetera, are the result of accidents."

Hume wrote, "there is no self, no individual. There is a continuation of thought."

Freud wrote, "I have found little that is 'good' about human beings on the whole. In my experience most of them are trash."

McNeil Dixon wrote, "the most successful slave trader operating out of Liverpool was Sir John Hawkins. He kidnapped some 75,000 natives from their homes in West Africa. The name of his slave ship was 'The Jesus.'"

And Shakespeare — of ten thousand hopeless phrases — his shortest, "out, out, brief candle —"

Pessimism and despair mark the works of most artists. For

truth has always a sigh in it, even when it speaks hopefully. St. Paul wrote of "the liberty wherewith Christ hath made us free." And the ex-Pharisee adds, "being thus made free from sin, ye become the servants of righteousness."

These are vague words but they reveal a rueful truth — the contradictory desires of humans who want always to be free and at the same time to be the servants of something.

But the antidote for the bitter findings of artists is nearly always the artists themselves.

My seven in these pages were given to dismal and derogatory utterances. They communed with death and dark skies. But what a brightness was in them. It is this brightness I remember of them, and have tried to recount.

Artists, great and small, have been to me what people usually consider professional clergymen to be — spokesmen for divinity. I have had little curiosity about God in my life. His whims and problems have seemed to me too hopeless a guessing game for my penny's worth of brain. That He exists and runs a million universes, each containing a billion stars, is "fact" enough for me.

And fact, also, is the handful of artists present always on our planet and animating always our history.

All people are, presumably, supplied with souls invented by our Maker. The souls of artists are not necessarily better than those of the non-artist multitudes. But they are more visible, as birds in flight are more visible than those hugging their nests.

It is this visibility that I also have hoped to recount in writing of my seven artist friends.

Hecht, Ben
    Letters from Bohemia.

Wilmington Public Library
Wilmington, N. C.

RULES

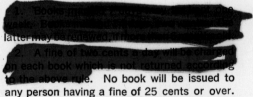

~~1. Books may~~ ~~one week.~~ ~~latter may be renewed, if~~

~~2. A fine of two cents a day will be charged~~ ~~on each book which is not returned according~~ ~~to the above rule.~~ No book will be issued to any person having a fine of 25 cents or over.

3. A charge of ten cents will be made for mutilated plastic jackets. All injuries books beyond reasonable wear and all losses shall be made good to the satisfaction of the Librarian.

4. Each borrower is held responsible for all books drawn on his card and for all fines ac-ing on the same.